BITCOIN REVOLUTION

LEARN HOW BITCOIN WORKS AND HOW TO INVEST. | WHY CRYPTOCURRENCIES WILL BE THE NEXT GLOBAL RESERVE CURRENCY.

WALLACE WHITTINGTON

CONTENTS

Introduction   v

1. How To Purchase Bitcoin   1
2. Wallet For Bitcoin   8
3. Buy Bitcoin Anywhere In The World   11
4. How to Cash Out Bitcoin: A Step-By-Step Guide   26
5. Guide To Buying Litecoin   33
6. The Difference Between Bitcoin And Litecoin   41
7. Bitcoin Mining   63

Afterword   75

© **Copyright 2021 by Wallace Whittington. All rights reserved.**

The purpose of this document is to provide accurate and reliable information on the subject and problem at hand. The book is sold to understand that the publisher is not obligated to provide accounting, legally authorized, or otherwise eligible services. If legal or professional advice is needed, a well-versed professional should be consulted.

A Committee of the American Bar Association and a Committee of Publishers and Associations also adopted and endorsed the Declaration of Principles.

No part of this document may be reproduced, duplicated, or transmitted in any manner, whether electronic or written. The recording of this publication is strictly forbidden, and preservation of this document is only permitted with the publisher's written permission. Both intellectual property rights are reserved.

The data presented here is said to be accurate and reliable. Any liability arising from the use or misuse of any procedures, processes, or instructions contained herein, whether due to inattention or otherwise, is solely and completely the responsibility of the recipient reader. Under no conditions will the publisher be held liable for any reparation, damages, or monetary loss incurred due to the information contained herein, whether directly or indirectly.

All copyrights not owned by the publisher belong to the authors.

The knowledge provided here is strictly for educational purposes and is therefore universal. The information is presented without some kind of contract or guarantee assurance.

The trademarks are used without the trademark owner's permission or backing, and the trademark is published without the trademark owner's permission or backing. All trademarks and labels mentioned in this book are their respective owners' property and are not associated with this.

INTRODUCTION

Bitcoin is a digital currency that was first introduced in January of 2009. It is based on ideas presented in a whitepaper by Satoshi Nakamoto, a mysterious and pseudonymous figure. The identity of the person or people behind the technology is still unknown. Bitcoin promises lower transaction costs than conventional online payment methods, and it is run by a decentralized authority, unlike government-issued currencies.

Bitcoin is a type of cryptocurrency. There are no physical bitcoins; instead, balances are kept on a public ledger that anyone can see. A vast amount of computational power is used to verify all bitcoin transactions. Individual bitcoins are not valuable as commodities since they are not distributed or guaranteed by any banks or governments. Although it is not legal tender, Bitcoin is extremely popular and has sparked hundreds of other cryptocurrencies known as altcoins. "BTC" is a common abbreviation for Bitcoin.

The bitcoin system is a collection of computers (also known as "nodes" or "miners") that run bitcoin's code and store its blockchain. A blockchain can be thought of as a series of blocks metaphorically. Each block contains a set of transactions. No one

Introduction

can cheat the system because all computers running the blockchain have the same list of blocks and transactions and can see all new blocks being filled with new bitcoin transactions transparently.

These transactions can be seen by anyone, whether or not they run a bitcoin "node." A bad actor will need to operate 51 percent of the computing power that makes up bitcoin to achieve a nefarious act. As of January 2021, Bitcoin had about 12,000 nodes, and this number is increasing, making quite an attack quite unlikely.

However, if an attack were to occur, bitcoin miners—those who participated in the bitcoin network with their computers—would most likely fork to a new blockchain, making the bad actor's effort put forth to achieve the attack a waste.

Public and private "keys," which are long strings of letters and numbers and connected by the mathematical encryption algorithm used to generate them, are used to keep track of bitcoin token balances. The public key (which is similar to a bank account number) serves as the made public's address and to which others may send bitcoins.

The private key (comparable to an ATM PIN) is intended to be kept private and is only used to authorize bitcoin transactions. A bitcoin wallet, a physical or digital device that enables bitcoin trading and allows users to monitor ownership of coins, should not be confused with bitcoin keys. The term "wallet" is misleading because bitcoin is never held "in" a wallet but rather decentralized on a blockchain.

1
HOW TO PURCHASE BITCOIN

Investing in Bitcoin may seem difficult initially, but it becomes much simpler once you break it down into stages. Purchasing Bitcoin is becoming easier by the day, and the trustworthiness of exchanges and wallets is increasing.

- Bitcoin's value stems from its use as a store of value and payment mechanism and its limited supply and low inflation.
- While it is almost impossible to hack Bitcoin itself, your wallet or exchange account can be hacked. This is why proper storage and security procedures are important.
- All that is needed to invest or trade Bitcoin is an account on an exchange, though additional safe storage practices are recommended.

Before You Get Started

Several items are required for any aspiring Bitcoin investor. You'll need a cryptocurrency exchange account, personal identity documents, a secure Internet connection, and a payment system if you're using a Know Your Customer (KYC) network. Separating your wallet from your exchange account is also a good idea. This route accepts bank accounts, debit cards, and credit cards as payment types. Specialized ATMs and peer-to-peer (P2P) exchanges are also options for getting Bitcoin. However, as of early 2020, Bitcoin ATMs increasingly required government-issued identification.

To buy bitcoin, you'll need a digital wallet, personal identification documents, a secure internet connection, a cryptocurrency exchange, and a method of payment.

Privacy and security are major concerns for Bitcoin investors. Even if there are no Bitcoins, boasting about large holdings is usually not a good idea. Anyone who gets their hands on the private key to a Bitcoin public address can approve transactions. Although private keys should be kept private, criminals may try to steal them if they learn large holdings. Keep in mind that everybody can use the balance of a public address device. As a result, keeping large investments at public addresses that aren't linked to the ones used for transactions is a good idea.

The blockchain's transaction history is accessible to anyone, including you. Personal information about users is not publicly reported on the blockchain, even though transactions are. Only a user's public key appears next to a Bitcoin blockchain transaction, making transactions private but not anonymous. In some respects, bitcoin transactions are easier and more traceable than cash, but they can also be used anonymously.

This is a significant distinction. According to international researchers and the FBI, Bitcoin blockchain transfers to users' other online accounts, such as digital wallets, can be tracked. Anyone who wants to open a Coinbase account, for example, must provide identification. When that person purchases Bitcoin, it is linked to their name. If they send it to another wallet, it can be traced back to the Coinbase transaction connected to the account holder's name. Since Bitcoin is legal in the United States and most developed countries, many investors should be unconcerned.

Step 1: Choose an Exchange

Signing up for a cryptocurrency exchange allows you to buy, sell, and keep cryptocurrency. Users are generally advised to use an exchange to deposit their cryptocurrency into a personal wallet for safekeeping. On some exchanges and brokerage sites, this is prohibited. For those who trade Bitcoin or other cryptocurrencies regularly, this feature may be irrelevant.

Exchanges for cryptocurrencies come in a variety of shapes and sizes. Some exchanges allow users to remain anonymous and do not require them to enter personal information due to the decentralization and individual autonomy ethos of Bitcoin. The exchanges that make this possible are usually self-contained and decentralized, which means there is no single point of control. To put it another way, if a regulatory body suspects criminal activity, there is no CEO and no individual or group to investigate.

Although these programs can be used for malicious purposes, they also provide services to the unbanked. This category includes refugees and those who live in countries with little or no government or banking infrastructure. To open a bank or investment account, state identification is required. Some argue that because unbanked people already have a way to save money and use it to get out of poverty, these programs' benefits outweigh the risk of illicit use.

Currently, the most widely used types of exchanges are not decentralized and require KYC. In the United States, these exchanges include Kraken, Coinbase, Gemini, and Binance U.S., to name a few. The number of features offered by each of these exchanges has significantly increased. Coinbase, Kraken, and Gemini all offer Bitcoin and a growing number of altcoins. These three methods are arguably the most straightforward in the entire industry for getting started with cryptocurrency. Binance is geared for the more seasoned trader, with more advanced trading features and a wide range of altcoins.

It's important to use safe internet practices when opening a cryptocurrency exchange account. This requires the use of two-factor authentication and the development of a unique and long password containing a mix of lowercase, capitalized, special, and numeric characters.

Step 2 : Integrate Your Exchange with a Payment Method

Once you've decided on a program, you'll need to collect your records. These could include images of a driver's license, your social security number, as well as information about your employer and source of funds, depending on the exchange. The knowledge you'll need is likely to be determined by the area you reside in and the laws that govern it. The procedure is similar to that of opening a traditional brokerage account.

You can buy and sell bitcoin and deposit the money directly into your bank account by connecting your wallet to your bank account.

After the exchange has checked your identity and legitimacy, you can now connect a payment option. You may connect your bank account or a debit or credit card to the exchanges mentioned above directly. While it is possible to purchase cryptocurrency with a credit card, it is usually advised against doing so due to cryptocurrencies' volatility.

Although Bitcoin is legal in the United States, some banks are skeptical of the concept and may decline to make deposits to cryptocurrency-related websites or exchanges. While most banks accept these deposits, double-check that your bank accepts deposits at the exchange you want to use.

Similar fees apply to deposits made with a checking account, debit card, or credit card. For example, Coinbase charges 1.49 percent for bank accounts and 3.99 percent for debit and credit cards, making it a good exchange for newcomers. Before deciding on an exchange or which payment option is best for you, it's critical to understand the fees associated with each payment option.

Step 3: Make a Purchase

After choosing an exchange and connecting a payment form, you can now buy Bitcoin and other cryptocurrencies. In recent years, cryptocurrency and cryptocurrency exchanges have grown in popularity. Exchanges have grown dramatically in terms of liquidity and feature set. What was once considered a scam or questionable has grown into something trustworthy and legitimate.

Cryptocurrency exchanges have advanced to the point that they now provide almost identical features to their stock brokerage counterparts. Once you've found an exchange and connected a payment method, you're ready to go.

Cryptocurrency exchanges also offer a wide range of order forms and investment options. Market and cap requests are accepted by almost every cryptocurrency exchange, and some also accept stop-loss orders. Of the exchanges mentioned above, Kraken has the most order types. On Kraken, you can place market, cap, stop-loss, stop-limit, and take-profit limit orders.

Aside from various order types, exchanges frequently offer clients the option of setting up recurring investments, which allow them to dollar cost average into their chosen investments. Coinbase, for example, lets users schedule transactions for the next day, week, or month. To buy Bitcoin or other cryptocurrencies, all you have to do is open an account on a cryptocurrency exchange. Still, there are a few other steps to take for added security and safety.

Step 4: Proper Storage

Bitcoin and other cryptocurrency wallets are a safe way to keep digital assets. Keeping your cryptocurrency in your wallet rather than on an exchange means that your funds' private key is only accessible to you. It also enables you to store funds outside of an exchange, lowering the risk of your funds being stolen if the exchange is compromised.

Bitcoins are a form of digital currency that must be stored in a digital wallet.

Although most exchanges offer wallets to their users, protection is not their top priority. We don't recommend using an exchange wallet for massive or long-term cryptocurrency holdings.

Some wallets come with a larger number of options than others. Some only accept Bitcoin, while others accept several altcoins. You can also swap one token for another in certain wallets.

When it comes to choosing a Bitcoin wallet, you have a lot of options. The first thing you can learn about crypto wallets is the difference between hot wallets (online wallets) and cold wallets (paper or hardware wallets).

COLD WALLETS

A cold wallet is simply a wallet that is not linked to the internet and poses a significantly lower risk of being hacked. These wallets are also known as hardware wallets or offline wallets.

These wallets store a user's private key on a device that isn't connected to the internet, and they can have software that runs in the background so that the user can access their portfolio without risking their private key. Offline, a paper wallet is also the safest place to store cryptocurrency. A paper wallet can be printed from several different websites. It then produces public and private keys, which you can print out. You can only get cryptocurrency from these addresses if you have the private key on a piece of paper. Many people laminate these paper wallets and store them in a safe deposit box at their bank or in their home safe. These wallets are best for high security and long-term investments because you can't easily sell or swap Bitcoin stored in them.

A hardware wallet is a form of cold wallet that is more widely used. A hardware wallet is a device that stores a user's private keys on the internet on a USB drive. This has many advantages over hot wallets, including the fact that it is immune to viruses on the user's computer. With hardware wallets, your private keys never come into touch with your network-connected computer or potentially compromised applications. These devices are also open source, enabling the world to vote on their protection rather than a company declaring it safe to use.

The best place to store Bitcoin and other cryptocurrencies are in a cold wallet. Setting them up, on the other hand, normally necessitates a little more experience.

A smart way to set up your wallets is to have three of them: a buying and selling exchange account, a hot wallet for small to medium amounts of crypto you want to trade or sell, and a cold hardware wallet long-term storage of larger holdings.

HOT WALLETS

"Cold" wallets are another term for online wallets. Hot wallets are digital wallets that operate on internet-connected devices such as laptops, smartphones, and tablets. Since these wallets produce the private keys to your coins on these internet-connected devices, this may pose a risk. While a hot wallet can be very useful for quickly accessing and transacting with your money, storing your private key on an internet-connected computer makes it more vulnerable to hacking.

While it might seem impossible, people who use these hot wallets without sufficient security risk getting their funds stolen. This is a natural occurrence that can manifest itself in several ways. It's not a good idea, for example, to brag about how much Bitcoin you have on a public forum like Reddit while using little to no security and keeping it in a hot wallet. These wallets, however, can be made to be secure if precautions are taken. Strong passwords, two-factor authentication, and secure internet browsing should all be needed.

These wallets are best for storing small amounts of bitcoin or cryptocurrencies that you are actively trading on an exchange. A hot wallet works in the same way as a checking account. According to traditional financial wisdom, you can keep just your discretionary money in a bank account and invest the remainder in savings or other investment vehicles. The same can be said for hot wallets. Hot wallets include mobile, laptop, network, and exchange account custody wallets.

As previously mentioned, exchange wallets are custodial accounts provided by the exchange. This wallet type owner does not have access to the private key to the cryptocurrency deposited in this wallet. If the exchange was hacked or if your account was compromised, your funds would be lost. The phrase "not your key, not your coin" is frequently heard in cryptocurrency forums and groups.

2
WALLET FOR BITCOIN

What is a Bitcoin Wallet, and How does it work ?

A Bitcoin wallet is a piece of software that stores Bitcoins. Bitcoins are not technically processed anywhere. Every person with a balance in a Bitcoin wallet has a private key (secret number) that corresponds to its Bitcoin address. Bitcoin wallets allow users to send and receive Bitcoins while also granting them ownership of their Bitcoin balance. Bitcoin wallets come in a variety of shapes and sizes. Desktop, tablet, internet, and hardware are the four major categories.

• A Bitcoin wallet is a software program for storing and exchanging Bitcoins rather than a physical object.

• A private key protects wallets. The key corresponds to the wallet's address.

• Laptop, tablet, internet, and hardware are the four styles of Bitcoin wallets.

Getting to Know Bitcoin Wallets

A digital wallet is another name for a Bitcoin wallet. A trader must first create a digital wallet to exchange Bitcoins. A Bitcoin wallet works in the same way as a physical wallet. Instead of physical currency, the wallet stores relevant data such as the encrypted private key used to access Bitcoin addresses and complete transactions. Desktop, tablet, internet, and hardware wallets are examples of Bitcoin wallets.

Desktop Wallets

Desktop wallets are mounted on a device and give the user full control over the wallet. Desktop wallets serve as a user's address for sending and receiving Bitcoins. They also offer the user the option of storing a private key. Bitcoin Core, MultiBit, Armory, Hive OS X, and Electrum are a few well-known desktop wallets.

Mobile Wallets

Mobile wallets are similar to desktop wallets in terms of functionality. Mobile wallets allow "touch-to-pay" and the scanning of a Q.R. code with near field communication (NFC) in physical stores. Mobile wallets include Bitcoin Wallet, Hive Android, and Mycelium Bitcoin Wallet. Bitcoin wallets are usually compatible with either the iOS or Android operating systems. Since there is a lot of malware masquerading as Bitcoin wallets, it's best to do some research before deciding which one to use.

Web Wallets

Web wallets enable users to access Bitcoins from any browser or mobile device. Since your private keys are stored online, you must choose your web wallet carefully. Famous web wallet providers include Coinbase and Blockchain.

Hardware Wallets

Hardware wallets, which store Bitcoins on a physical piece of equipment normally plugged into a computer via a USB port, are by far the most stable form of Bitcoin wallet. They are virtually resistant to virus attacks, and there have been few reports of Bitcoin theft. These are the only Bitcoin wallets that aren't secure, costing anywhere from $100 to $200.

Special Security Considerations for Wallets

Bitcoin wallets are high-value targets for hackers, so keeping them secure is important. Encrypting the wallet with a strong password and selecting a cold storage choice, which means storing

Bitcoins offline, are two precautions. It's also a good idea to back up your desktop and mobile wallets regularly, as problems with the wallet software on your computer or mobile device could wipe out your assets.

3
BUY BITCOIN ANYWHERE IN THE WORLD

There are various ways to buy Bitcoin in almost every country, including gift cards, bitcoin ATMs, local traders, brokers, and exchanges: This Chapter discusses how to purchase Bitcoin from any location on the planet.

Perhaps you've heard of Bitcoin, the bizarre cryptocurrency. The holy grail of Fintech, the future of finance, the payment revolution, the digital gold, the slayer of capital controls You may now be curious to learn more. The best way to learn is to do it yourself. Purchase a Bitcoin, use it to make a payment, save it in your digital wallet, and watch the price rise or fall. However, where do you get it? And how do you do it?

For many people, purchasing their first Bitcoin is a frightening experience. It appears to be extremely difficult. However, this is not the case. There are numerous options for purchasing your first Bitcoin quickly, conveniently, and comfortably.

Which one is the best is determined by your location and personal preferences.

TLDR:

1. Purchase Bitcoin with regular fiat currency.
2. If you have a wallet, you may purchase Bitcoins on a

Bitcoin exchange using a conventional payment system such as a credit card, bank transfer (ACH), debit card, interact, or E-transfer.

3. After that, the Bitcoins are moved to your cryptocurrency wallet.

However, before deciding on the best way to buy your first Bitcoin, you should consider the following factors:
- How much personal information are you willing to share?
- How would you like to pay?
- Where do you call home?

You should be able to easily determine which platform best suits your needs based on these factors.

This guide begins by outlining the choices for disclosing private information (or not disclosing it) and the payment methods available to you. The guide goes into the most popular ways to buy Bitcoin and an overview of many exchanges in various countries.

HOW TO PURCHASE BITCOIN FROM ANYWHERE ON THE WORLD

Private Information

Bitcoin is a financial instrument, and as such, most jurisdictions regulate it. Anti-Money-Laundering (AML) regulations are almost universally applied to websites selling Bitcoins or allowing users to buy and sell Bitcoins. To verify its customers' identity, most of these platforms must implement Know Your Customer (KYC) laws.

Since Bitcoin transactions are saved publicly available on the blockchain and can be traced back, the number of personal details you reveal while purchasing Bitcoins can have significant privacy implications.

There are many levels of KYC, each requiring you to reveal more personal details. The following is a list of grades, starting with the lowest:

- No Know Your Customer (KYC): If you don't have a KYC, the network or the Bitcoin seller does not know who you are. You don't need to display identification and pay with cash, Moneygram, Paysafecard, or Western Union. In some jurisdictions, buying Bitcoin without KYC is possible – for example, through P2P marketplaces such as LocalBitcoins, ATMs, or Gift Cards – but it is typically more costly than other alternatives.

• KYC Light: This KYC level uses your payment channel and/or phone numbers to identify you. Payment providers know your identity whether you pay through your bank account, PayPal, credit card, or another popular payment method. With KYC Light, you can buy a limited amount of Bitcoins on most sites, including direct exchanges, trading platforms, and marketplaces.

• Full KYC: In addition to using your phone number and bank account to check your identity, Full KYC requires you to have documents that prove your identity. A passport, an I.D. card, a driver's license, a utility bill, or a combination of all of these may be used. Some platforms require a notary or a trustworthy third party, such as your bank, to approve your identity documents; others are happy if you upload a photo of yourself holding your I.D. card or participate in the video verification process. There is typically no way around Full KYC if you want to spend significant sums of money or trade on exchanges.

WHAT IS THE BEST METHOD FOR PURCHASING BITCOIN?

Bitcoin is currency, but it can only be purchased by sending money to someone else. The more advanced your country's financial system is, and the better your country's financial system is, the easier it is to trade your money for Bitcoins.

The most significant impediment to Bitcoin trading is the movement of old fiat currency. Your Bitcoin will be acquired slowly and at a high cost if you use a slow and costly payment method. You can buy Bitcoins quickly if you use a fast channel.

Here's a partial, non-exhaustive list of popular ways to pay for Bitcoin:

• **Bank transfer** : Almost everybody is familiar with the good old Bank transfer. Typically, you send money to a Bitcoin seller and receive Bitcoins after the payments are completed using online banking. This takes 1-3 days in most countries. Direct debiting is not commonly recognized. Bank transfers are the only method of payment accepted by the majority of exchange platforms.

• **Credit Card** : Credit cards are one of the most widely used payment methods. However, credit cards are accepted by only a few direct commercial vendors. The explanation for this is that Bitcoin transactions cannot be reversed, whereas credit card transactions can. Vendors who accept credit cards have suffered losses as a result of this. Vendors often run the risk of people purchasing Bitcoin with stolen credit cards. Benefit from stolen credit card numbers with Bitcoins and use algorithms to reduce the danger.

• **PayPal:** Although a few sites support PayPal, most of them oppose it due to the same issues that credit cards have: PayPal transactions are easily reversed. The vendor can lose if this occurs after the buyer has moved the purchased Bitcoin to another wallet. This is why trading Bitcoins on eBay is a bad idea. However, some sites, including credit cards, accept PayPal.

• **Other Payment Channels** : (Sofort, iDeal, Skrill, etc.): Payment providers abound in the world of commerce. There are hundreds of them in the E.U. alone. A large number of direct exchanges supports a diverse selection of them. If you use a common supplier, such as Sofort in Germany or iDeal in the Netherlands, your domestic direct exchange is likely to accept it.

• **Private Payment Channels** (Cash, Western Union, Paysafecard, etc.): Most commercial platforms do not accept these payment methods. There are very few trading sites and almost certainly no direct exchanges that accept these payments. On p2p marketplaces, however, you will frequently find a seller who accepts cash or other private payment methods. An ATM where you can buy Bitcoins with cash might also be a good option.

WHAT IS THE MOST COST-EFFECTIVE METHOD OF PURCHASING BITCOIN?

We're getting closer to acquiring your Bitcoin now. In this section of our guide, we'll show you a few popular models for converting fiat money to digital cash – in Bitcoin. Each model has its own set of benefits and drawbacks.

• **Bitcoin ATM:** A Bitcoin ATM is perhaps the simplest and most private way to obtain Bitcoins. These machines where you can get money with your passport, you're familiar with them. Some companies, such as Lamassu, make Bitcoin ATMs where you can buy Bitcoin with cash. These devices' operators may use various KYC rules, ranging from cell phone authentication to biometric methods if they so choose. You will find a global map of these devices on Coin-ATM-Radar.com. Another type of ATM simply uses an existing ATM network to sell Bitcoins, such as those found in banks or train stations. This has been achieved in Switzerland, Ukraine, and Spain, for example. The majority of ATMs charge a fee of 3-6 percent or even more.

• **Gift Cards/Vouchers:** Another simple way to purchase Bitcoins is with a gift card or voucher. You go to a kiosk or another store and purchase a gift card or a voucher, then go to a website and enter the code on the card to get your Bitcoin. This approach is used in Austria, Mexico, and South Korea, among other places. Gift cards, like ATMs, are notorious for charging exorbitant fees.

• **Direct commercial exchanges/brokers:** These vendors are similar to the exchange offices found in airports, but they are interactive. They use an exchange to purchase Bitcoins and then sell them to customers. You go to a website, choose your payment method, pay, and receive Bitcoins at the platform's fixed rates. Most of these platforms require you to have your wallet, but others, such as Coinbase and Circle, allow you to save and spend your Bitcoins using a wallet they offer. Since such sites accept a wide range of payment methods, including credit cards and PayPal, they can be the quickest and most convenient way for newcomers to purchase their first Bitcoin. The fees for direct commercial exchanges range from 1% to 5%. Any of them benefit from the difference between buying and selling prices. Most charge additional fees for such payment methods, such as credit cards.

- **P2P-Marketplaces:** Buyers and sellers of Bitcoin meet and trade on P2P-marketplaces. The fees on these markets are modest, ranging from 0 to 1%; the spread is determined by the market's liquidity and the payment channel. You can take and make a bid, unlike direct: You decide on a price and then wait for someone to sell you a Bitcoin. This allows you to buy vast quantities of Bitcoin for relatively low prices. LocalBitcoins is the most well-known P2P marketplace. This global marketplace accepts various currencies and allows buyers and sellers to choose their preferred payment method. It's often used to encourage anonymous transactions, often at exorbitant rates. Bitcoin.de, the Eurozone's largest peer-to-peer (P2P) market, has strong liquidity and is a convenient way to convert Euro to Bitcoin. Bitsquare, a fully decentralized market that is nothing more than software that links people, is the third well-known P2P market.
- **Trading platforms:** Whether you want to buy large quantities of Bitcoin at low rates daily or trade with Bitcoins, you'll probably need an exchange platform. Exchanges serve as escrow for their customers, storing both Bitcoin and fiat money on their behalf. You can place your buy or sell orders here, and the exchanges' trading engine compiles these orders and offers from buyers and sellers and executes trades. Frequently, exchanges offer more trading options, such as margin trading. Fees and spreads are usually minimal. However, opening an account on an exchange can be difficult since it necessitates sharing personal details and trusting the exchange with your funds.

Exchanges, wallets, and banks have all been warned about.

Regardless of the proof of identity criteria, keep in mind that exchanges and wallets do not provide the same security level as banks.

For example, if the exchange goes out of business or is hacked, as was the case with the notorious failed exchange Mt Gox, there is sometimes no or restricted protection for your account.

In certain parts of the world, Bitcoin is not recognized as a legal tender, and authorities are sometimes at a loss regarding how to respond to robberies. Any larger exchanges have replaced customer funds after a fraud from the exchange, but they are not legally obligated to do so at this time.

WHAT IS THE BEST WAY TO BUY BITCOIN IN YOUR COUNTRY?

Worldwide: You can use local bitcoins, BitSquare, or Bitcoin ATMs almost anywhere on the planet. Although these are viable options, it is worthwhile to investigate other options available in your region.

NORTH AMERICA

The United States and Canada are two of the most famous Bitcoin markets. Buyers can purchase Bitcoins using several methods. Aside from LocalBitcoins and ATMs, direct vendors Coinbase, Circle, India Coin, the P2P-market Paxful, and the exchange Kraken are available in both countries.

UNITED STATES OF AMERICA

• Direct Exchanges : Two main sites, Coinbase and Kraken, make it simple to buy Bitcoins with low fees and store them in an online wallet. Both services support credit cards and bank transfers. Indacoin is another direct exchange network, but it lacks an integrated wallet. Another alternative, Expresscoin, allows you to buy Bitcoins with cash using Billpay.

• P2P-Markets : In addition to LocalBitcoins and Bitsquare, P2P-markets Bitquick and Paxful are available to consumers in the United States. On Bitquick, you pay by depositing cash into the seller's bank account; on Paxful, the seller can select from various payment methods, including PayPal, Western Union, credit and debit cards, gift cards, and more. Although Paxful's rates are normally very high, Bitquick charges a 2% fee.

• Exchanges : There are a few platforms to choose from if you want to buy Bitcoins with a Dollar on an exchange. Bitstamp, Coinbase's GDAX, and Bitfinex are the most common exchanges, followed by BTC-E, Kraken, and Gemini. While most exchanges only support bank transfers, BTC-E allows users to finance their accounts using credit cards and other payment providers such as PerfectMoney, Paysafecards, and others.

CANADA
• Direct : Both Kraken and Coinbase accept Canadian customers who can purchase Bitcoins using a bank transfer or a credit card and store them in the platform's online wallet. Customers from Canada may also use Indacoin. QuickBT and canadianbitcoins.com, for example, are websites where you can directly purchase Bitcoins for up to 150 Canadian Dollars using various payment methods such as INTERAC® Online and Flexepin Vouchers. Canadianbitcoin.com also accepts cash payments in person or by deposit.

• P2P : Canadian customers can purchase Bitcoins on foreign P2P markets such as Paxful and LocalBitcoin.

• Exchange : Canadian Dollars can be traded on some exchanges. The most well-known examples are Kraken and CoinSquare.

SOUTH AND CENTRAL AMERICA
Other than North America, Middle and South America were only recently introduced to Bitcoins, mainly in 2014/2015. Since most exchanges are fresh, investors must pay more in fees and spread because of the lower volume and liquidity.

In several South and Middle American countries, Satoshi Tango is a direct vendor for Brazil, Chile, Colombia, Costa Rica, Ecuador, El Salvador, Guatemala, Honduras, Mexico, Nicaragua, Panama, and Peru; Bitex. la is a direct vendor for Argentina, Chile, Colombia, and Uruguay.

Local bitcoins are available on the P2P market in most Latin American countries.

MEXICO
• Gift Cards : You can purchase Bitcoin gift cards at over 5.000 stores using the Chip-Chap.com app.

• Direct : Volabit.com enables users to purchase Bitcoin with MXN through bank transfers or cash deposits at OXXO, 7-Eleven, Banamex branches, and ATMs.

• Swap : Bitso.com is a Mexican exchange. Fees are steadily decreasing as trade volume increases, to as low as 0.1 percent, and the spread is small.

BRAZIL
• Direct : Brazilians can buy Bitcoins directly at Mercadobitcoin.com.br, a broker claiming to be Latin America's largest Bitcoin exchange.

• Exchange : FlowBTC is a major Bitcoin exchange in Brazil. People can buy and sell Bitcoins here. Ban transfers may be used to make deposits. Foxbit.com.br is a second big exchange.

ARGENTINA
• Direct : Ripio is a wallet application that enables users to purchase Bitcoins. Its unique feature is that it allows you to buy Bitcoins on credit and acts as a payment gateway for Bitcoin transactions.

In Venezuela, you can buy Bitcoin.

• Bitcoin exchange : SurBitcoin is Venezuela's own Bitcoin exchange.

CHILE
• Exchange : Chile has its Bitcoin exchange, SurBTC, which made international headlines after receiving government support. Bitcoins can be bought and sold here, and deposits in Chilean pesos can be made using local bank transfers.

EUROPE
• ATMs : The website coinatmradar.com has a list of hundreds of Bitcoin ATMs in Europe.

• Direct : Due to the hazy regulatory environment in the Eurozone, there is a slew of direct Bitcoin exchanges that accept a wide range of payment methods. The majority of these brokers charge their customers 0.5% to 5% fees depending on the payment channel and profit from the spread. While the sites mentioned above only sell Bitcoin and do not have an advanced online wallet, Coinbase and Circle both have an online wallet with the ability to buy Bitcoin using a bank transfer or credit card in most European countries.

• P2P-Markets : Except for Germany, LocalBitcoin is available in every Eurozone country. Bitcoin.de is a peer-to-peer (P2P) marketplace for the entire Eurozone, where users can buy and sell Bitcoins using SEPA transfers. Except for exchanges, Bitcoin.de is the cheapest way to purchase Bitcoins, with a 0.5% commission and a low spread.

• Exchange: Some exchanges serves the Eurozone. The most common exchange is Kraken, which Bitstamp and BTC-E follow. All exchanges require full КУС.

AUSTRIA,

Gift cards from bitcoin on. At, which are sold in several traffic shops, can be used to purchase Bitcoins by Austrian citizens. This is the most convenient but also the most expensive way of purchasing Bitcoins.

THE GERMANS

The Fidor-Bank is a good place for Germans to start buying Bitcoins. These online banks have partnered with Bitcoin.de and Kraken to make trading on these sites much quicker and easier. Fidor customers will get absolute КУС status and use the so-called ExpressTrade on Bitcoin.de right away. This allows them to purchase an infinite number of Bitcoins at low rates within minutes of contacting the website.

SPAIN

With Bit2Me.com and chip-chap.com, you can buy Bitcoins at thousands of ATMs in Spain.

EUROPE

Localbitcoins are available in almost every European country. Because of the favorable exchange rate between local currencies and the Euro, many European countries purchase Bitcoins through large European platforms (Kraken, bitcoin.de). Since high fees and widespread on small exchanges can add a significant premium to the price, it is often more cost-effective to convert the local currency to Euro and use Euro-platforms, which usually accept clients from all over Europe.

If a credit card is available, this is a convenient way to pay. Your credit card company profits from the currency exchange spread and charge; however, you can purchase Bitcoins quickly and easily.

THE UNITED KINGDOM

• Direct : U.K. residents can purchase Bitcoins directly from

Coinbase using bank transfers or credit cards. Many UK residents use bittylicious.com, which, in addition to bank transfers and credit cards, provides UK-specific payment options such as Paym and Barclays Pingit. However, depending on the payment method, the fees can be very high. A third broker that provides a direct exchange is

• Exchange : Coinfloor is the most common cryptocurrency exchange in the United Kingdom, followed by Kraken and Coinbase's GDAX.

• ATM : The Swiss national railway company, SBB, recently announced that Swiss people would be able to purchase Bitcoins at every ticket machine in every rail station. Cash or electronic cash is approved as a form of payment; credit cards are not accepted. Furthermore, bitconsuisse.ch operates Bitcoin ATMs in many locations in Switzerland.

• Direct : The Bitcoinsuisse.ch broker accepts cash and bank transfers for Bitcoin purchases. 247exchange.com has added the ability to purchase Bitcoins using Franken. Other direct exchanges, such as Coinbase and Circle, welcome Swiss customers but require them to pay in Euro.

POLAND

• Exchanges : BitMarket.pl, BitBay.net, and bitmaszyna.pl are all good options. There are three Bitcoin exchanges in Poland where you can buy Bitcoins with Zloty at reasonable rates.

NORWAY

• Direct : Cubits.com allows you to buy Bitcoins directly with NOK.

• Exchange : There is only one exchange in Norway, bitcoinsnorway.com. However, since the price is so low, consumers must pay a premium.

SWEDEN

• Direct : Sweden has two Bitcoin brokers, bt.cx and fybse.se, where you can purchase Bitcoin with SEK.

DENMARK

• Direct : Coinify.com is the only Danish exchange.

UKRAINE

- ATM : Using btcu.biz, you can purchase Bitcoins from any bank ATM around the world.
- Direct : Buy.kuna.io provides a direct Bitcoin to Hryvna exchange. btcu.biz is another direct trade.
- Exchange : Ukraine now has its Bitcoin exchange, kuna.io, for Hryvna.

NORWAY

- Direct: Cubits.com allows you to buy Bitcoins directly with NOK.
- Exchange: There is only one exchange in Norway, bitcoinsnorway.com. However, since the price is so low, consumers must pay a premium.

RUSSIA

Just a few exchanges and brokers remain in Russia due to the ambiguous legal status of Bitcoin. Localbitcoins seem to be used by a large number of people.

- Direct : matbea.com is a Bitcoin for Ruble direct seller. It necessitates the use of a phone number to register.
- BTC-E is the most popular exchange for trading Rubel and Bitcoin. It collaborates with several payment providers to allow funds to be deposited.

ASIA

Asia is the fastest-growing Bitcoin market. On exchanges in China, Japan, and South Korea, there is a brisk trade with Bitcoins, while Arabian countries like the Emirates are mostly Bitcoin-free. The best options in these countries are to locate an ATM or a seller on LocalBitcoins.

- **Exchanges in China** : China has the world's most liquid Bitcoin exchange landscape. Huobi, OKCoin, and BTC China are the exchanges with the most trading volume. Since these exchanges have no fees, the spread is extremely narrow. Aside from that, there are several other exchanges.

JAPAN

- Direct : Bitflyer.jp is the most common direct Yen, exchange broker. The broker charges very low fees and provides a wide range of verification degrees, from E-Mail to complete KYC.

- Exchange : Three exchanges serve the Japanese market: Quoine, Coincheck, and Kraken. Though they cannot compete with Chinese exchanges in terms of liquidity, they provide a decent service for purchasing Bitcoins at a low cost.

THAILAND
- Direct : bitcoin.co.th is a Bitcoin broker in Thailand. Coins.co.th, another dealer, offers a convenient online wallet.
- Exchange: Thailand now has its Bitcoin exchange, bx.in.th.

KOREA
- Direct and ATM : coinplug.com provides several options for purchasing and selling Bitcoins. They have two unique ATMs in Seoul, allow Bitcoin purchases in thousands of ATMs across the country through a partnership with an ATM manufacturer, and offer the option to buy Bitcoins with various gift cards.
- Exchange : South Korea has a well-developed exchange, korbit.co.kr, that offers Bitcoin trading and wallets for all devices and remittance services. Coinplug.com also has an exchange.

INDIA
- Direct: Unocoin.com, India's largest Bitcoin vendor, addresses buying, selling, saving, and sending Bitcoin. Zebpay.com, another major Bitcoin platform in India, provides a similar service. These two sites, like any other exchange in India, need identity verification.
- Exchange : Coinsecure.in is a wallet and an exchange in one.

THE PHILIPPINE
In the Philippines, you can buy Bitcoins on a wide range of platforms.
- Gift cards : You can use prepaidbitcoin.ph to redeem voucher cards purchased in various locations in the Philippines.
- Direct : buybitcoin.ph is a Bitcoin and coin vendor.
- Another Ph. Coins.ph accepts various payment methods, including bank deposits, online transactions, and store coupons available nationwide.
- Exchanges : The Philippines has two Bitcoin exchanges, coinage.ph and BTCexchange.ph.

TURKEY

Although Bitcoin is not controlled in Turkey, there appears to be increasing strain on Bitcoin companies following the failed coup and increased government restrictions.

• Gift-card : Bitupcard.com allows you to purchase a Bitcoin-redeemable voucher online.

• Direct : koinim.com is a website that allows Lira users to purchase Bitcoin and Litecoin directly.

• Exchange : The first Bitcoin exchange in Turkey is BTCTurk.com. You can buy and sell Bitcoins on this site. BTCTurk recently had issues with its bank account, and there were rumors that it would have to shut down. However, it appears to be operational at this time.

MIDDLE EAST
ISRAEL

• Direct : Bits of Gold is Israel's first Bitcoin forum. You can buy and sell Bitcoins directly here.

• Bitcoin exchange : Bit2C is the largest Bitcoin exchange in Israel.

• Other : Citizens of the United Arab Emirates can buy Bitcoins directly on bitoasis.net; in Kuwait, you can buy Bitcoins on bitfils.com; in Vietnam, you can buy Bitcoins the broker bitcoinvietnam.com.vn and the exchange vbtc.vn; in Malaysia, coinbox.biz and coins.my offer an online wallet and an easy way to buy and sell Bitcoins, respectively, while oinhako.com is a wallet with the option Bitcoins can also be purchased in Indonesia at bitcoin.co.id. Taiwanese citizens can purchase, sell, and use Bitcoins on maicoin.com.

OCEANIA
AUSTRALIA

• Direct : There are many direct Bitcoin vendors in Australia: Btradeaustralia.com accepts Poli-Payments, buyabitcoin.com.au accepts cash deposits in banks, cointree.com.au accepts all payment options, coinloft.com.au accepts both payment options and Flexepin vouchers, and bitcoin.com.au allows the purchase of Bitcoin by depositing cash at kiosks.

- Exchange: Australia has two exchanges: independentreserve.com and coinspot.com.au.

NEW ZEALAND
- Direct : You can buy Bitcoins through online bank transfers at coined.co.nz and bank deposits at buybitcoin.co.nz. Coinhub.nz provides further payment options, including cash deposits at ATMs and tellers, as well as PayPal. mybitcoinsaver.com provides a wallet and the ability to invest in Bitcoins daily through automated bank transfers.
- Bitcoin exchange : There are two Bitcoin exchanges in New Zealand. The spread on bitnz.com is reasonably broad, while nzbcx.com offers better rates.

AFRICA
In comparison to the rest of the world, Africa has a low acceptance rate for Bitcoin and just a few exchanges. In several countries, searching LocalBitcoins to find a local vendor is a good idea if no exchanges exist.

- Bit-X and ice3x.com are the two Bitcoin exchanges in South Africa (Ice Cube).

NIGERIA
- You can also exchange Bitcoins on Bit-X in Nigeria. You can also buy Bitcoins with bank transfers on nairaex.com, and buy coins with debit cards or paga on bitpesa.co.

TANZANIA
- In Tanzania, you can buy Bitcoins with bank transfers through bitpesa.co.

UGANDA
- Bitpesa.co allows Ugandans to purchase Bitcoins using MTN or Airtel Money.

ZIMBABWE
- Bitcoinfundi.com appears to be based in Zimbabwe, but the prices are shown in US dollars.

Purchasing bitcoins isn't always as easy as newcomers think. The good news is that the number of choices is growing, and it is becoming simpler.

4

HOW TO CASH OUT BITCOIN: A STEP-BY-STEP GUIDE

- Do you prefer the simplest or the cheapest method?
- Do you want the funds deposited into your bank account or transferred to your PayPal account?
- How long do you want to have to wait for your money?
- What currency do you exchange your Bitcoin for?

These are some of the questions you'll have to answer for yourself. So, take a look at the methods for cashing out bitcoin mentioned below and determine which is best for you.

Exchanges of third-party brokers

An exchange is referred to as a third-party broker. Most cryptocurrency exchanges do not allow you to deposit funds with fiat currency, but a few do.

This is how it works: you deposit your Bitcoin into the exchange, then request a fiat currency withdrawal once the exchange has received your Bitcoin. A bank (wire) transfer is the most common method of doing so.

You must withdraw to the same bank account that you deposited to ensure that brokers do not violate money-laundering laws. If you've never deposited fiat on a broker exchange before, you'll almost certainly need to make (at least) one first.

I understand how irritating this can be... But that's how things are.

If you plan to cash out your Bitcoin via a broker exchange (such as Coinbase), the money will usually arrive in your account in 1-5 days. Payments are made via SEPA for EU customers (withdrawals paid in Euros). When selling Bitcoin for USD, however, brokers usually use the SWIFT payment form.

And that's how to cash out Bitcoin using a broker exchange — skip ahead to the next segment for instructions.

Let's look at how to sell Bitcoin for cash using a peer-to-peer network if you'd prefer a more anonymous and time-saving method!

Peer-to-peer (P2P)

If you don't want to wait three days to cash out your Bitcoin, a peer-to-peer selling site like LocalBitcoins could be a good option.

When selling Bitcoins to others on LocalBitcoins, you have the option of choosing which payment method the buyers can use. There are some of them:

• Cash deposit : You may request that the buyer make a cash deposit into your bank account. Before issuing your Bitcoins to them, you should always ask for proof of identification and proof of payment.

• Money Transfer : You can request a bank transfer payment from the buyer. Before attempting this method of cashing out Bitcoin, make sure to obtain proof of the buyer's identification. You can give them the Bitcoins once you've earned money.

• Meet in person for cash : You will meet with a local buyer who will pay you in cash for your Bitcoins.

If you know what you're doing, P2P selling is healthy. However, it's important to be wary of con artists. Because of their escrow service, LocalBitcoins provides a high degree of security. This locks your Bitcoins until you receive confirmation from the buyer that payment has been made.

I'm sure you're still unsure what an escrow is, so let me give you an example:

1. John wishes to purchase one Bitcoin. He looks for sellers in his own country because he is from the United Kingdom.

2. John notices that Mike is selling 1 Bitcoin for a reasonable price and allows bank transfer as a payment method.

3. John sends Mike a request for 1 Bitcoin, which he accepts.

4. Mike deposits his single Bitcoin into the escrow account. This is where John's Bitcoin is held until he transfers the funds to Mike.

5. John deposits the agreed-upon amount into Mike's account.

6. Once Mike receives the invoice, he releases the Bitcoins from the escrow and sends them to John's account.

That concludes our discussion. You now know how to trade Bitcoin for cash on a peer-to-peer (P2P) exchange.

Using a Broker Exchange to Cash Out Bitcoin

Now that you understand the differences between the two most common methods, I'll show you how to convert Bitcoins to cash using broker exchanges!

Coinbase is a cryptocurrency exchange.

The most famous broker exchange for buying and selling Bitcoin is Coinbase. They handle more Bitcoin transactions than any other broker and have a huge 13 million-strong customer base.

• Withdrawal Methods : You can exchange Bitcoins for cash on Coinbase, which you can deposit into your bank account. Only a bank account that you used to buy cryptocurrency on Coinbase can be used to cash out your Bitcoin. So, if you haven't already, I suggest starting with a small amount of cryptocurrency.

• Charges : Fees vary depending on where your bank is based. A wire transfer, for example, costs $25 if you want to exchange Bitcoin for USD. If you live in the EU and have SEPA, this will just cost you $0.15!

• Withdrawal times are also dependent on the country in which your bank is located. Withdrawals from the United States usually take 4-6 business days, although withdrawals from the European Union take 1-3 business days.

Coinbase is a service that allows you to convert Bitcoin into cash.

I'll now show you how to cash out Bitcoin at Coinbase to make things a little simpler for you.

1. You must first create a Coinbase account, connect your bank account, and make a deposit. If you need assistance, please see our guide here. If you've already completed step 1, move on to step 2!

2. After you've created your Coinbase account, send your Bitcoin to your Coinbase Bitcoin address! To do so, go to the Accounts tab and open your Bitcoin wallet before clicking "Receive." Your Bitcoin Coinbase wallet address will then be shown. This is the address to which you should submit your Bitcoin.

3. When you're ready, go to the top of the page and press Buy/Sell.

4. Next, choose Sell.

5. The wallet is the next step in the Bitcoin cashout process. Assuming you've sent your Bitcoin to your Coinbase wallet, your Bitcoin wallet and default fiat currency should appear here. Since I opened an account in the European Union, my deposit wallet is in Euros (EUR).

6. Depending on where you are, this will change. Customers in the United States, for example, can withdraw in USD, while those in Japan can withdraw in JPY.

Your withdrawal cap will also be shown. Your limits will be very high if you have already checked your account. If you need to increase this, go to See Limits and follow the extra verification instructions!

7. You must first convert your Bitcoin to your local currency before withdrawing. In my case, I'm converting Bitcoin to Euro (EUR). Enter the sum of Bitcoin you want to sell, and the equivalent in fiat currency will be updated.

8. Your funds will now be in your fiat currency wallet after you press Sell Bitcoin Instantly.

9. Alright, we've reached the end of the process for with-

drawing Bitcoin to your bank account. Click on withdraw from your fiat currency wallet (for example, EUR/USD/YEN). Your bank account information will be saved from when you first set it up. You now know how to use Coinbase to convert Bitcoin to USD, EUR, and other fiat currencies. Don't forget that there are a plethora of other brokers to choose from. Kraken is another common choice for Bitcoin sellers.

10. Another well-known exchange that accepts fiat currency deposits and withdrawals is Kraken. It's been around since 2011 and handles the majority of Bitcoin to Euro conversions. They do, however, accept other major currencies such as USD, CAD, and JPY!

• Withdrawal Methods : You can withdraw your Bitcoin to a nearby bank account if you want to convert it into cash with Kraken.

• Fees : Kraken's withdrawal fees are extremely low. A SEPA cash out, for example, costs just €0.09! It's also just $5.00 to sell Bitcoin for US dollars at a nearby US branch!

• Cash-out times : Kraken withdrawals take 1-5 business days to enter your bank account.

Using a Peer-to-Peer Exchange, convert Bitcoin to Cash

Let me show you how to cash out Bitcoin using a peer-to-peer exchange now that you know how to cash out Bitcoin using a broker. There are a few to choose from, but Local Bitcoins is the one I recommend the most.

LocalBitcoins was established in 2012 and now operates in nearly every country on the planet. So, no matter where you live, you should be able to sell your Bitcoin to buyers.

P2P has the advantage of allowing you to request any payment method you want. Here are some examples of the various payment options on LocalBitcoins:
• International Bank Wire
• Local Bank Transfer
• PayPal
• Skrill
• Payoneer

- Western Union
- Gift Vouchers
- Web Money
- Bank Cash Deposit
- Neteller

Sellers who understand how to cash out Bitcoin can also choose the price they want to sell their Bitcoin. You can do so by making an advertisement, for which you will be charged 1% of the total sale.

There are no fees if you sell to a customer who has specified the price they want to pay.

You may also leave reviews for the buyer or seller, similar to how you can on eBay. This ensures that you are protected when selecting a buyer. I just recommend selling to customers who have 100% positive reviews if you are a novice.

Local Bitcoins also allow you to remain anonymous (when using payment methods like web money or gift vouchers), especially if you protect your link with a stable and secure VPN. On the other hand, some sellers request new buyers' identification (those who have left no feedback).

Here's how to convert Bitcoin to cash using a peer-to-peer exchange, step by step:

How to Use LocalBitcoins to Cash Out Bitcoin

1. To begin, you must first create an account with Local Bitcoins. You can do so by going to this link.

2. Create a strong username and password. Your email address must also be entered and verified.

3. Once you've signed in, go to the top of the page and press Sell Bitcoins.

4. Finally, you must choose the country in which your ideal buyers are based. Of course, I suggest using your own country, but it is entirely up to you. In this case, I've chosen the United Kingdom. You'll also need to specify how much Bitcoin you want to sell.

5. As you can see, there are various ways to cash out your Bitcoin.

6. I'll show you how to cash out Bitcoin using PayPal in this example. As you can see, the buyer has a perfect rating of 100 percent and has completed over 1000 trades! This is an indication that the buyer is committed and trustworthy.

7. Enter your PayPal email address and confirm the amount of Bitcoin you want to sell. Then press the Send Trade Request button.

8. Your buyer will be notified if you want to sell your Bitcoins to them. You'll then transfer your Bitcoins to the LocalBitcoins escrow (remember how I explained an escrow earlier?). As a result, the buyer will not obtain your Bitcoins until you confirm that they have paid you.

9. You may receive notification from the buyer that the funds have been sent. Check that the funds have arrived in your PayPal account, then press Payment Received to complete the transaction.

You can practice trading using various payment methods once you've gained some experience with Local Bitcoins. The good news is that some payment methods allow you to sell your Bitcoins for a higher price, so it's worth learning how to use them.

Setting up advertising is also a smart idea. Even though it will cost you 1% in fees, you can set your price and payment process. When customers want to buy from you, you will get a notification in this situation.

LocalBitcoins is just one of many peer-to-peer exchanges that allow you to cash out your Bitcoin. The most important thing to keep in mind is that the exchange has an escrow, and you can never give your Bitcoin to a buyer until they have paid!

5
GUIDE TO BUYING LITECOIN

Where to Buy Litecoin and How to Purchase Litecoin

This is largely dependent on where you are trying to buy Litecoin from and the mode of payment. This is because different 'territories' (countries and states) have different laws, and as a result, certain countries are unable to use certain Litecoin exchanges.

However, location isn't the only consideration when determining where to purchase Litecoin. There are three major factors to consider (in addition to the location/country of origin):
- Payment Method
- Country of Origin
- Fee Payments

First, consider how your payment method influences your decision...

Method of Payment

Platforms for Credit or Debit Cards

Buying Litecoin is easy, but some people can find it difficult due to how they pay for their Litecoin. Coinbase, a US-based website, allows you to buy Litecoins with a credit or debit card if you have one.

CoinMama, which is accessible from 188 countries, is another website that accepts credit cards. BitPanda, a crypto service located in the European Union, is another choice.

Platforms for Bank Transfers

BitPanda and Coinbase are two of the most user-friendly platforms for purchasing Litecoins via bank transfer.

Transfers from Coinbase will take up to five to seven working days in the United States and one to three days in the European Union. For bank transfers, Coinbase charges an average fee of 1.49 percent.

BitPanda, on the other hand, only accepts bank transfers from within the European Union.

So, if you're a US citizen looking to buy Litecoin via bank transfer, I recommend checking out Coinbase!

Before we get into the different ways you can buy Litecoins with cash or PayPal, let's talk about protection.

Never store your Litecoin on a cryptocurrency exchange (like Coinbase, Binance, etc.). Often move all of your Litecoin from your exchange to an offline wallet, a hardware wallet (like the Trezor).

Litecoin Purchases with Cash

There used to be no direct way to buy Litecoin for cash unless you met a guy down the bar who had Litecoin, and he wanted to trade his Litecoin for cash, but that doesn't sound very reliable...

Bitcoin ATMs are available, but they do not accept Litecoin. You might buy Bitcoin for cash and then exchange it for Litecoin electronically, just like many other options.

CoinFlip, on the other hand, has developed a multi-crypto ATM system that allows for Litecoin cash transactions! LTC has a cash-out feature that allows you to sell your LTC for cash.

The problem is that they're only available in the United States, and even then, there are only around thirty of them in the entire country.

Litecoins can be purchased with PayPal.

Some exchanges accept PayPal. One such platform is Cryptex24. You can choose your currency, enter the amount to be transferred, and then click "Exchange Now" to send the money, and you'll get your Litecoin within 0-4 hours of the transaction is accepted.

PayPal also made it illegal for cryptocurrency exchanges to allow the payment method. However, Cyptex24 isn't your typical exchange, and the transfer process is a good example of that.

Litecoin Purchases with Crypto

This is one of the most straightforward methods for purchasing Litecoin. If you already have Bitcoin in your wallet and have signed up, you can simply exchange LTC (Litecoin's symbol) for BTC (Bitcoin). The LTC/BTC pair is common, as is the LTC/ETH (Ether) pair!

Binance is one of the most famous and well-known cryptocurrency exchanges. In comparison to most other trading exchanges, their fees are also very modest! If you want to buy Litecoin with Bitcoin or Ethereum, this is the exchange I suggest.

Originating Country

There are federal and territorial 'locks on some sites.' Since payment methods are dependent on country-by-country partnerships, this is the case.

The easier it is to form a partnership with a country that is more "established." Coinbase is available in the United Kingdom, the United States, the European Union, Singapore, Australia, the United Arab Emirates, and Canada.

These laws are focused on exchanges that adhere to the legal requirements of local jurisdictions and countries. As a result, US customers must have different details than a German resident.

Since there is no uniform norm, exchanges must abide by the countries' electronic payment laws they wish to trade.

Charges

You should be aware of the various fees that apply and how they affect your Litecoin investments.

First and foremost, there is the miner tax. They're in Bitcoin, Ethereum, and Litecoin. This part is inevitable — regardless of which exchange you use, it will be the same.

Then there's the exchange fee to consider. Exchanges charge a commission or fee for each transaction executed on their platform in return for their services.

Comparing Litecoin Exchanges is a great way to find out where to buy Litecoin.

CoinMama, BitPanda, and Coinbase are three examples of broker exchanges (places that you can buy crypto with fiat). These are also the places to go if you want to buy Litecoin with a credit or debit card! Let's take a look at their benefits and drawbacks:

BitPanda is a cryptocurrency exchange.

The Benefits

Thanks to its compliance with EU money transfer rules, it is one of the largest brokerage crypto exchanges in the Eurozone.

Skrill, Debit and Credit Cards, Bank Giro Payments, SEPA, and other payment channels are all accepted, making purchasing Litecoin a breeze!

Disadvantages

It can only be purchased in the Eurozone.

It has an astringent verification procedure that must be followed before trading and exchanging. It has a complicated fee structure that adds to the difficulty of the experience.

Coinbase

The Benefits

Coinbase is a trading site as well as a brokerage firm. It has an excellent reputation and offers complete exchange rate services. It's extremely user-friendly!

Coinbase accepts money transfers and credit/debit card payments as payment types.

Disadvantages

Unlike other sites that cover 100+ countries, Coinbase is only available in 33 countries. Coinbase isn't available in every country.

Furthermore, Coinbase's verification tests are extremely stringent! The ID tests you complete determine your account limits.

CoinMama

The Benefits

CoinMama accepts a wide range of payment methods, including debit and credit cards, Western Union, and MoneyGram. This ensures that people who don't have access to conventional banking will use the portal.

The platform is available in every country and can be accessed from anywhere! Verification is, therefore, less of an issue than for other suppliers.

Disadvantages

CoinMama's fees are higher than those of other vendors, and it does not offer Litecoin. The main problem with CoinMama is that it does not allow bank transfers.

Many exchanges, like CoinMama, will not let you buy Litecoin. Instead, you'll need to purchase a different cryptocurrency (such as Bitcoin or Ether) and then pass it to a trading exchange to purchase Litecoin.

Let's take a look at each phase of the process to see how to buy Litecoin on some of the most common platforms.

Coinbase is the best place to buy Litecoin.

Coinbase allows you to buy Litecoin with your fiat currency (USD, EUR, etc.). Let's get started! It's beginner-friendly, so let's get started!

The first step is to create a Coinbase account, which you can do on your computer or by downloading the Coinbase app from the App Store (iOS) or Play Store (Android) (Android).

Your Coinbase account can be linked to your bank account, credit card, or even debit card.

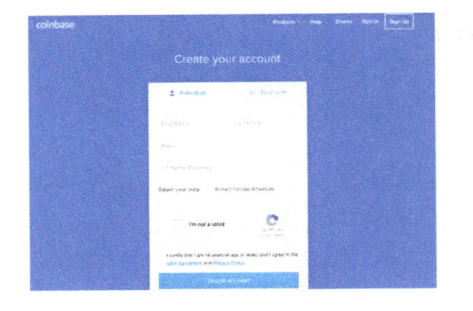

You'll need to double-check if they're your bank accounts or credit cards. After you've completed these steps, you'll be able to buy (and sell) Litecoin.

The next step is to purchase Litecoin.

On your Android or Apple smartphone, open the app. Scroll down to Litecoin on the homepage. Select the graph by clicking on it. You'll be taken to the next screen.

Owing to security restrictions, screenshots are not permitted on the next two windows. But it's very easy. The graph is on the next page, and below it are two blue buttons that say buy and sell. Select 'purchase' from the drop-down menu.

When you get to the buy tab, you can choose your payment method and the amount of fiat you want to spend. After that, you can purchase Litecoin.

It's as simple as that on Coinbase!

BitPanda is a great place to buy Litecoin.

BitPanda allows you to purchase Litecoin. The first move is to create a BitPanda account, which you can do by downloading the BitPanda app from the Apple App Store or Google Play. This will provide you with a secure method of purchasing Litecoin. To set up your account and buy your first Litecoin, follow these measures.

You will need to create an account. To create a simple account, you'll need to follow the on-screen instructions.

BitPanda requires all users to register to comply with Eurozone regulations. There are three stages, each of which has a time limit. The most expensive choice is Gold Verification, but it removes account limits.

For this method to function, you'll need your identification documents and access to a webcam.

You'll have full access to your trading account once you've registered and checked your account. Your starting point is the home screen (shown above).

Let's go ahead and buy some Litecoin on BitPanda.

You can now buy Litecoin with the funds you want to add from your EUR/LTC wallet transaction after you've selected Litecoin from the cryptocurrencies.

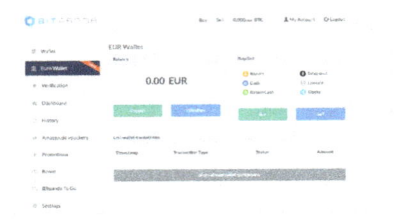

The processing time can also differ depending on the degree of account verification (so bear that in mind).

Purchasing Litecoin on BitPanda is as easy as that!

6
THE DIFFERENCE BETWEEN BITCOIN AND LITECOIN

A Comparison of Bitcoin and Litecoin

The public's interest in cryptocurrencies has shifted dramatically over the last few years. Investor interest in cryptos has risen dramatically since the turn of the century. The main subject of this attention has been Bitcoin, which has long been the most well-known brand in cryptocurrencies, unsurprising. It was the first digital currency to gain widespread acceptance.

Hundreds of other cryptocurrencies have entered the market since the launch of Bitcoin in 2009.1 While it has become increasingly difficult for digital coins to stand out in such a crowded field, Litecoin (LTC) is one non-Bitcoin cryptocurrency that has managed to hold its own. LTC is currently the sixth-largest digital currency by market capitalization, trailing only Bitcoin.

• Bitcoin and Litecoin are both digital currencies. Bitcoin, which was established in 2009, is the most famous cryptocurrency; Litecoin, which was founded two years later, is one of its main competitors.

• Bitcoin's market cap is $1 trillion as of March 2021, while Litecoin's is $13.7 billion.2

- Litecoin can produce more coins and has a faster transaction speed than Bitcoin. These are primarily psychological benefits for investors and have no bearing on the currency's value or usability.
- Bitcoin and Litecoin use cryptographic algorithms fundamentally different: Bitcoin uses the longstanding SHA-256 algorithm, while Litecoin uses the newer Scrypt algorithm.

Bitcoin and Litecoin have a lot in common.

On the surface, Bitcoin and Litecoin appear to be very similar. They are both decentralized cryptocurrencies at their most basic stage. Unlike fiat currencies like the US dollar or the Japanese yen, which depend on central banks for value, circulation control, and legitimacy, cryptocurrencies are decentralized. They rely solely on the network's cryptographic integrity for value, circulation control, and legitimacy.

Litecoin was founded in 2011 by former Google engineer Charlie Lee, who announced the launch of the "lite version of Bitcoin" via a message on a prominent Bitcoin forum. Litecoin was seen as a reaction to Bitcoin from the start. Indeed, Litecoin's creators have claimed for years that their goal is to build the "silver" to Bitcoin's "gold."

As a result, Litecoin adopts many of the features of Bitcoin that Lee and other developers thought were useful in the earlier cryptocurrency while also changing certain elements that the development team thought could be enhanced.

Work Samples

The fact that both Bitcoin and Litecoin are proof of work ecosystems is a significant similarity. That is to say, the process by which both cryptocurrencies are mined—that is, created, authenticated, and then added to a public ledger or blockchain—is fundamentally the same.

Transactions and Storage

Many of the essential elements of transacting with Bitcoin and Litecoin are also very similar for an investor. Both of these cryptocurrencies can be purchased on a cryptocurrency exchange or mined with a mining rig. To be safely stored between transactions, both require a digital or cold storage "wallet."

Furthermore, the values of both cryptocurrencies were shown to be highly volatile over time, depending on a variety of factors such as investor interest and government regulations.

Bitcoin vs. Litecoin: What's the Difference?

Capitalization of the market

The market capitalization, or total dollar market value of all outstanding coins, is one region where Bitcoin and Litecoin vary significantly.

The total amount of all bitcoins in existence is about $1 trillion as of March 2021, making Bitcoin's market cap more than 70 times that of Litecoin, which has a total value of $13.7 billion.2 If you consider Bitcoin's market cap to be big or low depends mostly on your historical context. When we remember that the market capitalization of Bitcoin was just $42,000 in July 2010, the current figure seems incredible.

Bitcoin also outnumbers all other digital currencies as a network. Given that Bitcoin is so far larger than all other digital currencies in existence at this moment, its closest rival is Ethereum, the second-largest cryptocurrency, with a market cap of approximately $212 billion.2 Therefore, the fact that Bitcoin has a considerably higher valuation than Litecoin is not surprising.

Distribution

Another significant distinction between Bitcoin and Litecoin is the total amount of coins that each cryptocurrency produces. This is where Litecoin sets itself apart. The Bitcoin network will never hold more than 21 million coins, while the Litecoin network can hold up to 84 million.

While this appears to be a major benefit for Litecoin in principle, its real-world implications may be minor. This is because both Bitcoin and Litecoin can be divided into almost infinitesimal numbers. The smallest amount of Bitcoin that can be transferred is one hundred millionth of a bitcoin (0.00000001 bitcoins), also known as one "satoshi."

Regardless of how high the general price of an undivided single Bitcoin or Litecoin rises, users of either currency should have no trouble buying low-cost products or services.

Litecoin's greater number of maximum coins could give a psychological advantage over Bitcoin due to the lower price for a single unit.

In November 2013, IBM executive Richard Brown raised the possibility that some users may prefer transacting in whole units rather than in fractions of a unit, a possible benefit for Litecoin.5 But even assuming this is true, the problem may be solved by simple software changes implemented in the digital wallets through which Bitcoin transactions are made.

As Tristan Winters points out in a Bitcoin Magazine post, "The Psychology of Decimals," common Bitcoin wallets such as Coinbase and Trezor now provide the option to show the Bitcoin value in terms of official (or fiat) currencies such as the U.S. dollar. This can help circumvent the psychological aversion to dealing with infractions.

Transaction Speed

While theoretically, transactions occur instantaneously on both the Bitcoin and Litecoin networks, time is taken to validate such transactions by other network participants. Litecoin was developed to prioritize transaction speed, and that has proven an asset as it has increased in popularity.

According to information from Blockchain.com, the Bitcoin network's average transaction confirmation period (the time it takes for a block to be validated and added to the blockchain) is currently just under nine minutes per transaction. However, this can vary widely when traffic is high. The equivalent figure for Litecoin is approximately 2.5 minutes.

In theory, this difference in confirmation time may make Litecoin more appealing for merchants. For example, a vendor selling a product in exchange for Bitcoin will need to wait nearly four times as long to validate the payment as if the same product were sold in exchange for Litecoin. Merchants, on the other hand, can also accept transactions without waiting for any confirmation.

The security of zero-confirmation transactions is a hot topic of discussion.

Transaction Speed

While transactions on the Bitcoin and Litecoin networks are theoretically instantaneous, it takes time for those transactions to be validated by other network participants. Litecoin was created to prioritize transaction speed, which has proven to benefit as the currency has increased in popularity.

According to Blockchain.com, the average transaction confirmation period (the time it takes for a block to be checked and added to the blockchain) on the Bitcoin network is currently under nine minutes per transaction. However, this can vary greatly when traffic is high. Litecoin's equivalent figure is approximately 2.5 minutes.

This difference in confirmation time might, in theory, make Litecoin more appealing to merchants. A retailer selling a product in exchange for Bitcoin, for example, will have to wait nearly four times as long to receive a payment confirmation as if the same product was sold in exchange for Litecoin. On the other hand, merchants can often choose to approve transactions without waiting for confirmation. The safety of zero-confirmation transactions is a point of contention.

Algorithms.

The use of different cryptographic algorithms is by far the most fundamental technical discrepancy between Bitcoin and Litecoin. The long-standing SHA-256 algorithm is used by Bitcoin, while Scrypt is a relatively new algorithm used by Litecoin.

The effect of these various algorithms on the method of mining new coins is their most functional significance. Confirming transactions in both Bitcoin and Litecoin necessitates a significant amount of computing resources. Miners are members of the currency network who devote their computational power to verifying other users' transactions. These miners are compensated for their efforts by receiving units of the currency they have mined.

SHA-256 is a more complicated algorithm than Scrypt, but it allows for more parallel processing. As a result, Bitcoin miners have become increasingly advanced in recent years to mine bitcoins as efficiently as possible. The use of Application-Specific Integrated Circuits (ASICs) is the most popular approach for Bitcoin mining.

Unlike the basic CPUs and GPUs that came before them, these are hardware systems customized to mine Bitcoins. As a result, Bitcoin mining has become completely out of reach for the average person unless they enter a mining pool.

Scrypt, on the other hand, was created to be less vulnerable to the custom hardware solutions used in ASIC-based mining. Many observers believe that Scrypt-based cryptocurrencies like Litecoin are more open to users who also want to participate in the network as miners. Although some companies have released Scrypt ASICs, Litecoin's vision of more easily accessible mining remains a reality, as the majority of Litecoin mining is still performed on miners' CPUs or GPUs.11

LITECOIN VS. BITCOIN FAQS

What Is Litecoin Used For?

Given the uproar surrounding its prices and market capitalization, Litecoin may exist primarily to be bought and sold, to paraphrase an old traders' joke about soybeans. However, Litecoin, like all cryptocurrencies, is a form of digital currency. Individuals and organizations may use it to make purchases and move funds between accounts.

It's suitable for smaller, daily transactions because of its relative speed and low cost. Without using an intermediary such as a bank, credit card business, or payment processing service, participants work directly.

Can You Convert Litecoin to Bitcoin?

You can swap litecoins for bitcoins and vice versa, just as you can do with fiat currencies like dollars for pounds or yen for euros. Swapping one for the other is usually not a concern since they are both leading and extremely liquid cryptocurrencies.

To do so, you'll need a cryptocurrency trading or exchange

network or trading app account. The amount you'll get from the conversion is, of course, determined by the current exchange rates for and currency.

Is it possible to submit Litecoin to a Bitcoin wallet?

Since you can't submit Litecoin to a Bitcoin address (even though they're in the same wallet), it's crucial to recognize cryptocurrency conversion. You will lose money if you do so. If you have seed backups for the keys that allow you to access your account, recovery can be possible, but it's difficult.

Is Litecoin on the verge of displacing Bitcoin?

It's anyone's guess if Litecoin would ever surpass Bitcoin as the most famous cryptocurrency. Bitcoin is the first digital currency, and many people associate it with cryptocurrencies in general—almost it's a generic word like Kleenex is for facial tissue.

If any other cryptocurrency were to dethrone Bitcoin, Ethereum (currently ranked second) or one of the other higher-ranked currencies would be the most probable candidates. Litecoin's fundamentals, however, are liked by some analysts. In a 2018 article for The Motley Fool, stock picker Sean Williams wrote, "Litecoin can process transactions faster than bitcoin, and its faster block time means that it can handle more power than bitcoin," adding, "it most certainly has the tools to drive bitcoin aside and become the go-to medium of exchange for digital currency users."

Although Bitcoin and Litecoin are currently the gold and silver of the cryptocurrency space, history has shown that the status quo in this fast-moving and still-developing industry will shift in a matter of months. It's unclear if the cryptocurrencies we've become acquainted with will maintain their prominence in the months and years ahead.

You may have heard the word "blockchain," the record-keeping technology behind the Bitcoin network, whether you've been following finance, trading, or cryptocurrencies over the last ten years.

• A blockchain database is a special kind of database.
• The storage method varies from that of a traditional

database; blockchains store data in blocks that are then chained together.

- As new information is received, it is entered into a new block. If the block has been filled with data, it is chained onto the previous block, resulting in a chronological chain of data.
- A blockchain can store various data, but the most popular use has been as a transaction ledger.
- In the case of Bitcoin, blockchain is used in a decentralized manner, meaning that no one individual or community has power—rather, all users have control collectively.
- Decentralized blockchains are permanent, meaning the data entered cannot be changed. This ensures that transactions in Bitcoin are permanently registered and accessible to everyone.

What is Blockchain?

While blockchain appears to be complicated, and it can be, its core concept is rather easy. A database, or blockchain, is a form of digital ledger. To comprehend blockchain, it is essential to first comprehend what a database is.

A database is a collection of data stored on a computer device in an electronic format. Database information, or data, is usually organized in table format to make searching and filtering specific information easier.

What's the difference between a spreadsheet and a database when it comes to storing data?

Spreadsheets are structured to store and access limited quantities of data for a single individual or a small group of people. On the other hand, a database is structured to hold much greater volumes of data that can be accessed, filtered, and manipulated by any number of users at the same time.

Large databases do this by storing information on servers comprised of powerful computers. To provide the computing power and storage space required for multiple users to access the database simultaneously, these servers may often be constructed using hundreds or thousands of computers. Although anyone can access a spreadsheet or database, a company is often owned and maintained by a designated person who has full control over its functions and the data it contains.

So, what's the difference between a blockchain and a database?

Storage Structure

The way data is structured significantly between a traditional database and a blockchain. A blockchain is a digital ledger that organizes data into groups called blocks, each containing a collection of data. When a block is filled, it is chained onto the previous filled block, creating a " blockchain "data chain." All new knowledge that comes after the newly added block is compiled into a newly created block, added to the chain until it is filled.

A database organizes information into tables, while a blockchain organizes information into chunks (blocks) linked together. Both blockchains are databases as a result, but not all databases are blockchains. When applied in a decentralized manner, this system creates an irreversible data timeline. When a block is filled, it becomes permanent and part of the timeline. When a block is attached to the chain, it is assigned an exact timestamp.

Attributes of Cryptocurrency

Decentralization

It's helpful to think about blockchain in terms and how it's been applied by Bitcoin to better understand it. Bitcoin, like a database, relies on a network of computers to store the blockchain. This blockchain is simply a form of the ledger that records every Bitcoin transaction ever made for Bitcoin. In the case of Bitcoin, unlike most databases, these machines are not all housed under one roof, and each computer or group of computers is run by a single person or group of people.

Consider a corporation that maintains a server with 10,000 computers and a database that contains all of its clients' account records. This organization owns a warehouse that houses all of these computers under one roof and has complete control over them and the information they hold. Similarly, Bitcoin is made up of thousands of computers. Still, each computer or group of computers that holds its blockchain is located in a different part of the world and is run by different people. Nodes are the machines that make up the Bitcoin network.

The blockchain of Bitcoin is used in a decentralized manner in this model. On the other hand, private, centralized blockchains exist in which all of the machines that make up the network are owned and run by a single individual.

Each node in a blockchain has a complete record of all data stored on the blockchain since its inception. The data for Bitcoin is the complete history of all Bitcoin transactions. If a node's data contains an error, it may use the thousands of other nodes as a point of reference to fix it. This way, no single node in the network can change the data it contains. As a result, the past transactions in each block of Bitcoin's blockchain are unchangeable.

If one user tampers with Bitcoin's transaction record, all other nodes can cross-reference each other, making it easy to find the node that has the incorrect data. This method aids in the establishment of a precise and straightforward sequence of events. A blockchain can store various information, such as legal contracts, state identifications, or a company's product inventory. For Bitcoin, this information is a list of transactions, but it can also contain various information, such as legal contracts, state identifications, or a company's product inventory.

The majority of the decentralized network's computing power will have to agree on the changes to alter how the system operates or the information stored inside it. This means that any improvements that do take place are in the majority's best interests.

Transparency

Due to Bitcoin's decentralized nature, all transactions can be transparently viewed using a personal node or blockchain explorers, which enable everyone to see transactions as they happen in real-time. Every node has a copy of the chain that is updated as new blocks are added and checked. This means that if you wanted to, you could follow Bitcoin wherever it goes.

Exchanges, for example, have been compromised in the past, resulting in the loss of all Bitcoin stored on the exchange. Although the hacker can remain unidentified, the Bitcoins they stole are easily traceable. It would be known if the Bitcoins stolen in any of these hacks were transferred or spent somewhere.

Is Blockchain a Safe Investment?

In many ways, blockchain technology addresses the issues of protection and trust. First and foremost, new blocks are often stored in sequential and chronological order. That is, they are often added to the blockchain's "top." If you look at the Bitcoin blockchain, you'll notice that each block has a spot on the chain called a "height," which had reached 656,197 blocks as of November 2020.

It is difficult to go back and change the contents of a block after it has been added to the end of the blockchain unless the majority agrees. Each block has its hash and the hash of the block before it and the time stamp listed earlier. A math function converts digital data into a string of numbers and letters, resulting in hash codes. The hash code changes if the information is changed in some way.

Here's why that matters in terms of protection. Let's say a hacker tries to change the blockchain to steal Bitcoin from the rest of the world. If they changed their single copy, it would no longer match the copy of anyone else. When anyone else compares their versions, they'll notice that this one stands out, and the hacker's version of the chain will be discarded as illegitimate.

To succeed in such a hack, the hacker will have to simultaneously manipulate and change 51 percent of the blockchain copies, ensuring that their new copy becomes the majority copy and, therefore, the agreed-upon chain. An attack like this would cost a lot of money and energy because they'd have to redo all of the blocks. After all, the timestamps and hash codes would be different now.

The cost of pulling off such a feat will almost certainly be impossible, given Bitcoin's network's scale and how quickly it is increasing. This would not only be prohibitively costly, but it would also be futile. Such actions would not go unnoticed by network members, who would note such significant changes to the blockchain. Members of the network will then fork off to a new, unaffected version of the chain.

This would cause the value of the attacked version of Bitcoin to plunge, rendering the attack futile since the bad actor would have a worthless asset. If a malicious guy attacked Bitcoin's latest fork, the same thing would happen. It's designed this way so that participating in the network is much more financially rewarding than targeting it.

BLOCKCHAIN VS. BITCOIN

Blockchain aims to allow for the recording and distribution of digital data without editing it. Stuart Haber and W. Edwards first proposed blockchain technology in 1991. Scott Stornetta, two researchers, tried to build a method that could not be tampered with when it came to recording timestamps. Blockchain didn't have its first real-world implementation until almost two decades later, with the introduction of Bitcoin in January 2009.

A blockchain is the foundation of the Bitcoin protocol. Bitcoin's pseudonymous founder, Satoshi Nakamoto, described the digital currency as "a new electronic cash system that's completely peer-to-peer, with no trusted third party" in a research paper introducing it.

The important thing to remember is that Bitcoin only uses blockchain to create a transparent ledger of payments; however, blockchain can theoretically be used to immutably record any number of data points. As previously stated, this may take the form of purchases, election votes, commodity inventories, state identifications, home deeds, and much more.

Currently, there are a plethora of blockchain-based ventures attempting to use blockchain for purposes other than transaction documentation. The use of blockchain as a voting system in democratic elections is a clear example. Because of the immutability of blockchain, fraudulent voting will become even more difficult.

For example, a voting scheme may be set up such that each

resident of a country receives a single cryptocurrency or token. Each candidate would then be assigned a unique wallet address, and voters would send their tokens or crypto to the address of the candidate they wish to support. Since blockchain is transparent and traceable, it eliminates the need for human vote counting and bad actors' potential to tamper with physical ballots.

BANKS VS. BLOCKCHAIN

Decentralized blockchains and banks are vastly different. Let's equate the banking structure to Bitcoin's blockchain implementation to see if it varies from the blockchain.

What is the Role of Blockchain?

Blocks on Bitcoin's blockchain, as we now know, store data about monetary transactions. However, it turns out that blockchain can also store data about other forms of transactions.

Walmart, Pfizer, AIG, Siemens, Unilever, and many other firms have also adopted blockchain technology. IBM, for example, has developed the Food Trust blockchain1 to monitor the path that food items take to reach their destinations.

Why are you doing this? Countless outbreaks of E. coli, salmonella, and listeria, as well as toxic chemicals inadvertently added to foods, have occurred in the food industry. It used to take weeks to figure out what was causing these outbreaks or what was causing people to get sick from what they were eating.

Brands can monitor a food product's journey from its origin to each stop it makes, and finally to its distribution, thanks to blockchain. If a food is found to be infected, it can be traced back to its source by each stop. Not only that, but these firms will now see what else they've come into contact with, potentially saving lives and allowing the issue to be identified much earlier. This is one example of a blockchain in action, but there are several other ways to incorporate a blockchain.

Banking and financial services

Banking is perhaps the industry that stands to gain the most from incorporating blockchain into its business operations. Financial institutions are only open five days a week during business hours. That means that if you want to deposit a check at

6 p.m. on Friday, you'll probably have to wait until Monday morning to see the funds in your account. Even if you make your deposit during business hours, it can take one to three days for the transaction to be verified due to the high volume of transactions that banks must process. Blockchain, on the other hand, is awake all the time.

Consumers can see their transactions completed in as little as ten minutes[2] by incorporating blockchain into banks, which is the time it takes to add a block to the blockchain, regardless of holidays or the time of day or week. Banks can now exchange funds between institutions more easily and safely, thanks to blockchain. The settlement and clearing process in the stock market industry, for example, can take up to three days (or longer if trading internationally), which means that the money and shares are frozen during that time.

Because of the large amounts involved, even a few days in transit will result in substantial costs and banks' risks. According to the European bank Santander and its research partners, the potential savings range from $15 billion to $20 billion per year[3]. Capgemini, a French consultancy, estimates that blockchain-based technologies could save customers up to $16 billion per year[4] in banking and insurance fees.

Currency

Blockchain is the foundation for cryptocurrencies like Bitcoin. The Federal Reserve is in control of the US dollar. A user's data and currency are legally at the discretion of their bank or government under this central authority scheme. If a user's bank is compromised, their personal information is exposed. The value of a client's currency may be jeopardized if their bank fails or if they reside in a country with an authoritarian government. Some of the banks that went bankrupt in 2008 were partly bailed out with taxpayer money. These are the concerns that led to the creation and development of Bitcoin.

Blockchain enables other cryptocurrencies to function without a central authority's need by distributing their activities through a network of computers. This not only lowers risk but also removes a lot of the transaction and processing costs. It can also provide a more secure currency with more applications and a larger network of individuals and institutions to do business, both domestically and internationally, for countries with unstable currencies or financial infrastructures.

For those who do not have state identification, using cryptocurrency wallets for savings accounts or as a means of payment is particularly important. Some countries may be in the midst of a civil war, or their governments may lack the necessary infrastructure to provide identification. Citizens of such countries may be unable to open savings or brokerage accounts, leaving them with no means of securely storing money.

Health-care

Health-care providers may use blockchain to store their patients' medical records safely. When a medical record is created and authenticated, it can be stored on the blockchain, giving patients evidence and assurance that the record cannot be altered. These personal health records could be encrypted and stored on the blockchain with a private key, meaning that only certain people can access them.

Records of Property

If you've ever visited your local Recorder's Office, you know how slow and time-consuming the process of recording property rights can be. A physical deed must now be sent to a government employee at the local recording office, who manually enters it into the county's central database and public index. Land arguments must be reconciled with the public index in the event of a property dispute.

This procedure is not only expensive and time-consuming, but it is also prone to human error, with each inaccuracy reducing the efficiency of property ownership monitoring. Scanning records and tracking down physical files in a local recording office may be obsolete thanks to blockchain. Property owners can assume that their deed is valid and permanently registered if stored and validated on the blockchain.

It can be virtually impossible to prove ownership of a property in war-torn countries or places with little or no government or financial infrastructure and no "Recorder's Office." Land ownership timelines might be defined straightforwardly and consistently if a group of people residing in such an area could use blockchain.

Smart Contracts

A smart contract is a computer code embedded in the blockchain to help promote, check, or negotiate a contract. Users agree to a set of conditions for smart contracts to work. The terms of the agreement are immediately carried out until those conditions are met.

Let's say a prospective tenant wants to lease an apartment using a smart contract. When the occupant pays the security deposit, the landlord offers to give the apartment's door code tenant. Both the tenant and the landlord must send their portions of the agreement to the smart contract, which would keep track of the door co code and automatically swap it for the security deposit on the lease's start date. The security deposit is refunded if the landlord fails to include the door code by the lease date. This will remove the costs and procedures associated with using a notary, third-party mediator, or attorneys.

Chains of Distribution

Suppliers may use blockchain to track the source of materials they buy, similar to the IBM Food Trust example. Along with popular labels like "Organic," "Local," and "Fair Trade," this will enable businesses to check the authenticity of their goods.

According to Forbes, the food industry is increasingly using blockchain to monitor the direction and protection of food during the farm-to-user journey.

Voting

As previously mentioned, blockchain could be used to aid in the creation of a modern voting system. As shown in the November 2018 midterm elections in West Virginia, voting with blockchain can reduce electoral fraud and increase voter turnout. Using blockchain in this way would make tampering with votes nearly impossible. The blockchain protocol will also ensure democratic accountability by reducing the number of people required to run an election and providing officials with near-instant results. There would be no need for recounts, and there would be no real risk that the result would be tainted by fraud.

THE BENEFITS AND DRAWBACKS OF BLOCKCHAIN

Despite its difficulty, blockchain's ability as a decentralized record-keeping system is almost limitless. Blockchain technology can have applications beyond those mentioned above, ranging from increased user privacy and protection to lower transaction fees and fewer errors. However, there are several drawbacks.

<u>Advantages</u>

• Increased precision by eliminating the need for human verification.

• Cost savings by obviating the need for third-party verification

• Decentralization makes it more difficult to tamper with data.

• Transactions are safe, convenient, and fast.

• Transparent hardware

• Provides residents of countries with insecure or underdeveloped governments with a banking option and a way to protect personal details.

<u>Drawbacks</u>

• Bitcoin mining has a significant technological expense.

• Transactions per second are low

• Use of illegal acts in the past

• Legislation

<u>Benefits of Blockchain</u>

Transaction Accuracy on the Blockchain A network of thousands of computers approves transactions on the blockchain network. This virtually eliminates human intervention in the verification process, resulting in lower human error and a more reliable data record. And if one of the computers on the network made a cryptographic error, it would only affect one copy of the blockchain. To spread to the rest of the blockchain, the mistake will have to be made by at least 51 percent of the network's computers, which is nearly impossible in a massive and network like Bitcoin's.

Reduced Costs

Consumers typically pay a bank to validate a transaction, a notary to sign a document or a minister to marry them. The blockchain removes the need for third-party authentication, as well as the costs that come with it. When businesses accept credit card payments, they must pay a small fee to banks and payment processing firms to process the transactions. On the other hand, Bitcoin has no central authority and only has a small transaction fee.

Blockchain doesn't keep all of its data in a single location. Instead, a network of computers copies and spreads the blockchain. Every device on the network updates its blockchain to represent a new block to the blockchain. Blockchain makes it more difficult to tamper with data by disseminating it through a network rather than storing it in a single central database. If a hacker obtained a snapshot of the blockchain, only a single copy of the data would be compromised rather than the entire network.

Transactions that are quick and easy

The settlement of transactions made through a central authority will take several days. For example, if you deposit a check on Friday evening, you can not see your account's funds until Monday morning. Blockchain operates seven days a week, 24 hours a day, and 365 days a year, while financial institutions operate during business hours, five days a week. Transactions can be done in as little as ten minutes, and after just a few hours, they are considered stable. This is especially useful for cross-border transactions, which take much longer due to time zone differences and the requirement that both parties confirm payment processing.

Transactions in Confidentiality

Many blockchain networks function as public databases, allowing anyone with an internet connection to access the network's transaction history. While users have access to transaction data, they do not have access to identifying information about the users who are conducting the transactions. It's a common misconception that blockchain networks like bitcoin are private when they're not.

Rather than their details, a user's unique code, known as a public key, is stored on the blockchain when making public transactions. A person's identity is always connected to their blockchain address if they made a Bitcoin purchase on an exchange that needs authentication. However, even when bound to a person's name, a transaction may not disclose personal details.

Secure Transactions

The blockchain network must verify the validity of a transaction after it has been registered. Thousands of computers on the blockchain scramble to verify that the purchase's details are right. The transaction is applied to the blockchain block after a device has checked it. The blockchain has its unique hash, as well as the hash of the previous block. The hashcode of a block changes when the information on it is changed somehow; however, the block's hashcode after it does not. Because of this disparity, changing details on the blockchain without warning is extremely difficult.

Transparency is essential.

The majority of blockchains are made up entirely of open-source software. This ensures that anyone with access to the internet can look at the code. This allows auditors to check the security of cryptocurrencies, including Bitcoin. This also implies that no real authority exists on who owns Bitcoin's code or how it is edited. As a result, everyone can propose system improvements or adjustments. Bitcoin will be upgraded if most network users accept that the latest version of the code with the upgrade is sound and worthwhile.

Banking the Unbanked

The ability for anybody, regardless of race, gender, or cultural context, to use blockchain and Bitcoin is perhaps its most significant feature. According to World Bank, nearly 2 billion adults lack bank accounts or other means of holding their money or assets. 5 Almost all of these people live in developing countries, where the economy is still in its infancy and money is king.

These individuals also receive small amounts of money that are paid in cash. They must then hide this physical cash in their homes or business places, leaving them vulnerable to theft or needless abuse. A bitcoin wallet's keys can be written down, saved on a cheap mobile phone, or even memorized if necessary. These solutions are more likely to be hidden than a small cash pile under a mattress for most people.

Blockchains of the future are also searching for ways to store medical records, property rights, and a host of other legal contracts in addition to being a unit of account for wealth storage.

Blockchain's Disadvantages

While the blockchain has many benefits, it also has many drawbacks when it comes to adoption. Today's roadblocks to blockchain technology adoption aren't only technological. For the most part, the real obstacles are political and legislative, not to mention the thousands of hours (read: money) of custom software design and back-end programming needed to incorporate blockchain into existing business networks. The following are some of the roadblocks to widespread blockchain adoption.

Technology Cost

Although blockchain can save users money on transaction fees, it is not a free technology. Bitcoin's "proof of work" scheme, for example, consumes a tremendous amount of computing resources to verify transactions. In the real world, the power generated by the bitcoin network's millions of computers is roughly equivalent to Denmark's annual electricity consumption. Mining costs, except hardware costs, are about $5,000$7,000 per coin, assuming $0.03$0.05 per kilowatt-hour energy costs.

Despite the high costs of bitcoin mining, consumers continue to increase their energy bills to validate blockchain transactions. That's because miners are compensated with enough bitcoin for their time and effort when adding a block to the bitcoin blockchain. However, miners will need to be charged or otherwise incentivized to verify transactions on blockchains that do not use cryptocurrencies.

Some solutions to these problems are starting to emerge. Bitcoin mining farms, for example, have been set up to use solar power, waste natural gas from fracking sites, or wind farm power.

Speed Inefficiency

Bitcoin is an excellent example of blockchain's potential inefficiencies. It takes about ten minutes for Bitcoin's "proof of work" method to add a new block to the blockchain. According to estimates (TPS), the blockchain network can only handle about seven transactions per second at that point. Other cryptocurrencies, such as Ethereum, outperform bitcoin, but they are still constrained by blockchain. For background, the legacy Visa brand can process 24,000 TPS.

For years, people have been working on solutions to this issue. Some blockchains can handle over 30,000 transactions per second right now.

Illegal Behavior

While the blockchain network's anonymity protects users from hacking and maintains their privacy, it also allows for illicit trade and operation. The Silk Road, an anonymous "dark web" drug marketplace that operated from February 2011 until October 2013, when the FBI shut it down, is perhaps the most well-known example of blockchain being used for illegal transactions.

Users may search the website without being monitored and make illegal Bitcoin and other cryptocurrency purchases using the Tor browser. According to current US regulations, financial service providers must collect information about their customers before they open an account, check each customer's identity, and ensure that customers do not appear on any list of confirmed or alleged terrorist groups. This method has both advantages and disadvantages. It helps everyone to access financial accounts, but it also makes it easier for criminals to transact. Many have argued that the positive uses of cryptocurrency, such as banking the unbanked, outweigh the negative uses, particularly because most criminal activity is still carried out with untraceable cash.

Regulation

Many people in the crypto community are worried about government oversight of cryptocurrencies. Governments could potentially make it illegal to own cryptocurrencies or participate in their networks, despite ending anything like Bitcoin is becoming extremely difficult and nearly impossible as its decentralized network develops.

As large corporations like PayPal continue to promote the ownership and usage of cryptocurrencies on their platforms, this issue has diminished.

What Does the Future Hold for Blockchain?

Blockchain, which was first proposed as a research project in 19917, is now in its late twenties. Blockchain, like most millennials its generation, has gotten a lot of press in the last two decades, with companies all over the world speculating about what the technology will do and where it will go in the future.

With many practical applications for the technology already being applied and explored, blockchain, at the age of twenty-seven, is gradually making a name for itself, thanks in no small part to bitcoin and cryptocurrencies. Blockchain, a buzzword on the lips of any investor in the country, promises to make business and government operations more accurate, reliable, stable and cost-effective by eliminating middlemen.

It is no longer a question of "whether" legacy businesses would adopt blockchain—it's a question of "when." As we enter the third decade of blockchain, it's no longer a question of "if."

7
BITCOIN MINING

What is Bitcoin Mining?

Cryptocurrency mining is time-consuming, costly, and only lucrative on rare occasions. On the other hand, many cryptocurrency investors are drawn to mining because miners are compensated with crypto tokens in exchange for their efforts. This may be because, like California gold prospectors in 1849, entrepreneurs regard mining as a divine gift. If you are technologically inclined, why not try it?

However, before you invest your time and money into mining, read this explanation to see if it's right for you. We'll concentrate on Bitcoin (we'll use "Bitcoin" to refer to the network or cryptocurrency as a term throughout, and "bitcoin" to refer to several individual tokens).

- You will raise cryptocurrency without having to pay for it through mining.
- Bitcoin miners are paid in Bitcoin to complete "blocks" of validated transactions and add them to the blockchain.
- The miner who discovers a solution to a complex hashing puzzle first receives a reward. The likelihood that a participant

will be the one to discover the solution is proportional to their share of the network's overall mining capacity.

• To set up a mining rig, you will need either a **GPU** (graphics processing unit) or an application-specific integrated circuit (ASIC).

A New Gold Rush

The promise of being paid with Bitcoin is a major draw for many miners. To be clear, you do not need to be a miner to own cryptocurrency tokens. You can purchase cryptocurrencies with fiat currency, swap them on an exchange like Bitstamp with another cryptocurrency (for example, Ethereum or NEO to buy Bitcoin), or gain them by shopping, writing blog posts on sites that pay users in cryptocurrency or even setting up interest-earning crypto accounts. Steemit is an example of a crypto blog site similar to Medium but allows users to reward bloggers with STEEM, a proprietary cryptocurrency. STEEM can then be exchanged for Bitcoin elsewhere.

Miners receive a Bitcoin reward as an incentive to help with mining's primary goal, legitimizing and tracking Bitcoin transactions to ensure their validity. Bitcoin is a "decentralized" cryptocurrency, meaning it is not regulated by a central authority such as a central bank or government, so these obligations are distributed to several users worldwide.

HOW TO MINE BITCOINS

Auditor miners are compensated for their efforts. They are in charge of ensuring that Bitcoin transactions are legitimate. Satoshi Nakamoto, the inventor of Bitcoin, devised this convention to keep Bitcoin users truthful. Miners help to avoid the "double-spending crisis" by checking transactions.

Double spending refers to a scenario in which a bitcoin owner spends the same bitcoin twice. This isn't an issue with real money: if you send someone a $20 bill to buy a bottle of vodka, you don't have it anymore, so there's no chance of them using it to buy lottery tickets next door. While counterfeit money is a possibility, spending the same dollar twice is not. According to the

Investopedia dictionary, "there is a risk that the holder will make a copy of the digital token and give it to a merchant or another party while holding the original."

Assume you have one $20 bill that is authentic and one $20 bill that is counterfeit. If you tried to spend both the genuine and false bills, anyone who looked at the serial numbers on both of them would find that they were identical, meaning that one of them was fake. A Bitcoin miner operates similarly, reviewing transactions to make sure users aren't spending the same bitcoin twice. As we'll see further down, this isn't a true analogy.

After checking 1 MB (megabyte) worth of bitcoin transactions, known as a "block," miners are entitled to be rewarded with bitcoin. Satoshi Nakamoto set the 1 MB limit, a contention source among miners, who believe the block size should be increased to accommodate more data, allowing the bitcoin network to process and verify transactions more quickly.

Note that a coin miner will receive bitcoin after verifying 1 MB of transactions; however, not everyone who verifies transactions will be paid out.

1MB of transactions can potentially be as little as one (though this is extremely rare) or as many as several thousand. It is dependent on the amount of data consumed by the transactions.

"So, even after all that work of checking transactions, I might not get any bitcoin in return?"

Yes, you are right.

To gain bitcoins, you must fulfill two requirements. One is a result of commitment, and the other is a result of chance.

1) You must check approximately 1MB of transactions. This is the most straightforward element.

2) You must be the first miner to solve a numerical problem with the correct answer or the nearest answer. Evidence of work is another name for this procedure.

"What exactly do you mean when you say 'the correct answer to a numeric problem'?"

The good news is that no advanced mathematics or

computation is needed. Miners aren't supposed to solve difficult mathematical problems, but that isn't the case. They're attempting to be the first miner to generate a 64-digit hexadecimal number (a "hash") that is either less than or equal to the target hash. It's essentially a guessing game.

The bad news is that its guesswork, but with the total number of potential guesses for each of these problems in the trillions, it's extremely taxing. Miners need a lot of computational power to solve a problem first. You'll need a high "hash rate" to mine successfully, which is calculated in megahashes per second (MH/s), gigahashes per second (GH/s), and terahashes per second (TH/s).

There are a lot of hashes there.

Cryptocompare provides a useful calculator for estimating how much bitcoin you might mine with your mining rig's hash rate.

<u>Bitcoin mining and circulation</u>

Mining serves another important function besides lining miners' pockets and maintaining the bitcoin ecosystem: it is the only way to release new cryptocurrencies into circulation. To put it another way, miners are essentially "minting" money. For example, there were approximately 18.5 million bitcoins in circulation as of November 2020. Miners were responsible for producing any single Bitcoin, except the coins minted by the genesis block (the first block, which Satoshi Nakamoto created). In the absence of miners, the Bitcoin network will continue to run and be usable. However, no new bitcoin will be produced. Bitcoin mining will end at some point, with the total number of bitcoins capped at 21 million according to the Bitcoin Protocol. However, since the rate at which bitcoins are "mined" slows over time, the final bitcoin won't be distributed until about 2140. This isn't to assume that all transactions will be scrutinized. Miners will have to verify transactions and be rewarded for their contributions to preserve the Bitcoin network's credibility.

Coin mining will grant you "voting" control when changes to the Bitcoin network protocol are proposed, in addition to the short-term Bitcoin payoff. To put it another way, miners have a say in how forking decisions are made.

HOW MUCH DOES A MINER MAKE?

Every four years, the incentives for bitcoin mining are halved. One block of bitcoin was worth 50 BTC when it was first mined in 2009. This was reduced to 25 BTC in 2012. By 2016, it had been cut in half again, to 12.5 BTC. The reward was halved again on May 11, 2020, to 6.25 BTC. November of 2020, the price of Bitcoin was about $17,900 per Bitcoin, which meant that completing a block would earn you $111,875 (6.25 x 17,900). 3 It does not seem to be a bad incentive to solve the complex hash problem mentioned above.

You may consult the Bitcoin Clock, which updates this information in real-time, to keep track of when these halvings will occur. Interestingly, bitcoin's market price has continued to correlate strongly with the reduction of new coins entering circulation over its existence. Because of the lower inflation rate, the shortage has increased, and prices have risen in response.

If you're curious about how many blocks have been mined so far, many websites, including Blockchain.info, will provide you with that information in real-time.

Is There Anything I Need To Mine Bitcoins?

People may have been able to compete for blocks with a standard at-home machine early on in Bitcoin's history, but this is no longer the case. This is because the complexity of mining Bitcoin fluctuates over time. The Bitcoin network aims to generate one block every 10 minutes to ensure the blockchain's smooth operation and ability to process and validate transactions. However, if one million mining rigs compete to solve the hash problem, they would most likely find a solution faster than ten mining rigs work on the same problem. As a result, every 2,016 blocks, or approximately every two weeks, Bitcoin evaluates and adjusts mining complexity. As more computing power is pooled to mine Bitcoin, the difficulty level of mining rises to maintain a consistent block production rate. The complexity level decreases as computing power decreases. To give you an idea of how much computational power is involved, consider that when Bitcoin first released in 2009, the difficulty level was one. It is more than 13 trillion dollars as of November 2019.

All of this means that miners must now invest in powerful computer equipment such as a GPU (graphics processing unit) or, more realistically, an application-specific integrated circuit to mine competitively (ASIC). These can cost anything from $500 to tens of thousands of dollars. Individual graphics cards (GPUs) are purchased by some miners, especially Ethereum miners, as a low-cost way to put together mining operations.

THE "EXPLAIN IT LIKE I'M FIVE" VERSION

The ins and outs of bitcoin mining are complicated enough as it is. Consider the following illustration of how the hash problem works: I tell three friends I'm thinking of a number between one and one hundred, and I write it down on a piece of paper and enclose it in an envelope. My friends do not have to guess the exact number; all they have to do is be the first to guess any number that is less than or equal to the one I'm considering. There is no limit on the number of guesses they will get.

Let's pretend I'm considering the number 19. They lose if Friend A guesses 21 because 21>19. Instead of 1619 and 1219, if Friend B guesses 16 and Friend C guesses 12, they've both technically arrived at viable answers. Even though Friend B's response was closer to the mark of 19, there is no "extra credit" for him. Consider the following scenario: I ask three friends to guess what number I'm thinking of, but I'm not thinking of a number between 1 and 100. Rather, I'm pondering a 64-digit hexadecimal number and asking millions of would-be miners. You can see how difficult it would be to guess the correct answer.

If B and C both respond at the same time, the ELI5 analogy fails.

Simultaneous responses are popular in Bitcoin, but there can only be one winning response at the end of the day. When multiple simultaneous responses are equal to or less than the target number, the Bitcoin network will choose which miner to honor based on a simple majority—51 percent. Typically, the miner who has completed the most work or verified the most transactions is the winner. After that, the losing block is referred to as an "orphan block." The term "orphan block" refers to a block that has not been added to the blockchain. Miners who have solved the hash problem but haven't checked the most transactions aren't paid in bitcoin.

What Does It Mean to Have a "64-Digit Hexadecimal Number"?

Here's an example of a number like this:
0000000000000000057fcc708cf0130d95e27c5819203e9f967ac56e4df598e

The above number has 64 digits. So far, it's been fairly simple to comprehend. As you might have noted, the number includes both numbers and letters from the alphabet. What is the reason for this?

Let's unpack the term "hexadecimal" to see what these letters are doing in the middle of numbers.

As you might be aware, we use the "decimal" scheme based on base ten. As a result, each digit of a multi-digit number has ten possibilities, ranging from zero to nine.

"Hexadecimal," on the other hand, refers to the base 16 system, as "hex" comes from the Greek word for six and "deca" comes from the Greek word for ten. Each digit in the hexadecimal system has 16 possible values. However, our numerical method only provides ten different ways to represent numbers (zero through nine). That is why you must insert letters, namely letters a, b, c, d, e, and f.

You don't need to calculate the total value of that 64-digit number if you're mining bitcoin (the hash). You don't need to measure a hash's total worth, I repeat.

So, what exactly are "64-digit hexadecimal numbers," and how do they relate to bitcoin mining?

Remember how I wrote the number 19 on a piece of paper and sealed it in an envelope for the ELI5 analogy?

The goal hash is the unknown metaphorical amount in the envelope in bitcoin mining terms.

Miners are guessing at the goal hash with those massive

computers and thousands of cooling fans. Miners make these guesses by making as many "nonces" as they can as quickly as they can. The secret to creating these 64-bit hexadecimal numbers I keep talking about is a nonce, which stands for "number only used once." A nonce in Bitcoin mining is 32 bits long, much smaller than the hash, 256 bits. The first miner to produce a hash that is less than or equal to the goal hash is credited with completing the block and receives 6.25 BTC as a reward.

You could theoretically obtain the same result by rolling a 16-sided die 64 times to generate random numbers, but why would you want to?

"How do I figure out what the goal hash is?"

All target hashes start with zeros, with a minimum of eight and a maximum of 63 zeros.

There is no minimum target, but the Bitcoin Protocol has set a maximum target. No goal can be higher than this:

00000000fff-f00000000000000000000000000000000000000000000000000000

Here are some examples of randomized hashes, as well as the requirements for determining whether they can contribute to miner success:

"How can I improve my odds of guessing the goal hash before someone else?"

You'd need to invest in a powerful mining rig or, more realistically, enter a mining pool, which is a collection of coin miners who pool their computing power and divide the bitcoin they mine. Mining pools are similar to Powerball teams, in which members purchase lottery tickets in bulk and plan to split the proceeds. Pools mine a relatively large number of blocks compared to individual miners.

To put it another way, it's purely a numbers game. You can't make a prediction based on previous target hashes or guess the pattern. At the time of writing, the most recent block's difficulty level is about 17.59 trillion, which means that every given nonce has a one in 17.59 trillion chance of generating a hash below the mark. Even with a super-powerful mining rig, you don't stand a chance if you're operating alone.

"How do I know if bitcoin is going to be successful for me?"

Miners must not only consider the costs of the costly equipment used to solve a hash problem. They must also know how much electricity mining rigs can generate massive amounts of nonces to pursue the solution. As of this writing, bitcoin mining is essentially unprofitable for most individual miners. Cryptocompare has a handy calculator where you can type in numbers like the hash and energy costs to estimate the costs and benefits.

WHAT ARE COIN MINING POOLS AND HOW DO THEY WORK?

The miner who discovers a solution to the puzzle first receives mining rewards. The probability that a participant will be the first to discover the solution is proportional to their share of the network's total mining power. Individuals with a small percentage of the mining power have a very slim chance of independently discovering the next block. For example, a mining card costing a couple of thousand dollars would represent less than 0.001% of the network's total mining power. With such a small chance of finding the next block, it could take a long time for that miner to find one, and as the difficulty increases, things become even more difficult. The miner's investment can never be recouped. Mining pools are the solution to this issue. Third-party mining pools manage and organize groups of miners. Miners can get a steady flow of bitcoin from the day they activate their miner by working together in a pool and sharing payouts among all participants. Blockchain.info has statistics on a few of the mining pools.

"I've crunched the numbers. Don't bother with mining. Is there a less time-consuming way to make money with cryptocurrencies?"

As previously stated, the simplest way to obtain bitcoin is to purchase it on one of the numerous exchanges. You may also use the "pickaxe technique" as an alternative. This is based on the adage that during the 1849 California gold rush, the smart investment was to make mining pickaxes rather than pan for gold. Alternatively, invest in the companies that make those pickaxes in today's terms. A company that manufactures Bitcoin mining equipment would be the pickaxe equivalent in the cryptocurrency world. Instead, you could look into companies that manufacture ASICs or GPUs, for example.

Is Bitcoin Mining a Legitimate Business?

The legality of Bitcoin mining is entirely dependent on your location. The concept of Bitcoin may pose a threat to fiat currency dominance and government control of financial markets. As a result, Bitcoin is completely illegal in some jurisdictions.

Bitcoin mining and ownership are legal in a growing number of countries. Algeria, Egypt, Bolivia, Morocco, Ecuador, Nepal, and Pakistan are just a few examples of countries where it is prohibited. 4 Overall, Bitcoin mining and use are legal in most parts of the world.

Risks of Mining

The risks associated with mining are frequently financial and regulatory. Mining, in general, is a financial risk, as previously stated. One could go to great lengths to purchase mining equipment worth hundreds or thousands of dollars only to see no return on their investment. However, by entering mining pools, this risk can be reduced. If you're thinking about mining but live in a region where it's forbidden, you should think twice. It is also a great idea to look into your country's cryptocurrency regulations and sentiment before purchasing mining equipment.

Another possible risk associated with the rise of bitcoin mining (and other proof-of-work schemes) is the increased energy consumption of the computer systems that run the mining algorithms. Although the performance of ASIC chips has improved significantly, the network's growth is outpacing technological advancement. As a result, there are questions about Bitcoin mining's environmental effects and carbon footprint. There are, however, attempts to reduce this negative externality by using carbon offset credits and finding safer and greener energy sources for mining operations (such as geothermal or solar). Another tactic is to switch to less energy-intensive consensus mechanisms like proof-of-stake (PoS), which Ethereum plans to do. However, PoS has its collection of disadvantages and inefficiencies.

AFTERWORD

For the past two years, Bitcoin has been firmly in the media spotlight. Even if Bitcoin is no longer relevant, cryptocurrencies have shown viable alternatives to institutionally backed internet transactions.

The number of daily Bitcoin transactions has increased this month. Over the short term, the number of transactions has risen while the price of Bitcoin has remained relatively stable, suggesting stable growth patterns. Still, bullish Bitcoin analysts are few and far between. Mastercard announced that it regards all anonymous Bitcoin transactions as "suspicious transactions," giving the technology an unavoidably dark impression.

Federal law enforcement agencies continue to be concerned about criminal activity and the use of Bitcoin in black markets on the "Deep Web." Bitcoin's success and anonymity make it a desirable option for criminals who depended solely on cash and unruly banks. When developed with a political agenda, technological innovations have appeared to be libertarian; most new applications and software developments have bolstered Bitcoin's anonymizing capabilities (Dark Wallet is the primary example). Tech advancements will continue to affect the government's

Afterword

ability to control Bitcoin and other virtual currencies, influencing potential policy decisions.

Although many people sought bitcoin currency to circumvent government regulation, the high rate of illegal activity via Bitcoin rendered regulation inevitable. In the last two years, the US government has accepted Bitcoin as a form of property and started to regulate it. By registering businesses that use Bitcoins, the government hopes to make illegal activity involving the currency more difficult.